1995

*The Institution of Theor*

*The Problems of Aesthetics* (co-editor, with Eliseo Vivas) 1953

*The New Apologists for Poetry* 1956

*The Tragic Vision: Variations on a Theme in Literary Interpretation* 1960

*A Window to Criticism: Shakespeare's Sonnets and Modern Poetics* 1964

*Northrop Frye in Modern Criticism* (editor) 1966

*The Play and Place of Criticism* 1967

*The Classic Vision: The Retreat from Extremity in Modern Literature* 1971

*Theory of Criticism: A Tradition and Its System* 1976

*Directions for Criticism: Structuralism and Its Alternatives* (co-editor, with L. S. Dembo) 1977

*Poetic Presence and Illusion: Essays in Critical History and Theory* 1979

*Arts on the Level: The Fall of the Elite Object* 1981

*The Aims of Representation: Subject/Text/History* (editor) 1987

*Words about Words about Words: Theory, Criticism, and the Literary Text* 1988

*A Reopening of Closure: Organicism against Itself* 1989

*Ekphrasis: The Illusion of the Natural Sign* 1992

# The Institution of Theory

Murray Krieger

The Johns Hopkins University Press
Baltimore and London

© 1994 The Johns Hopkins University Press
All rights reserved. Published 1994
Printed in the United States of America on acid-free paper

03  02  01  00  99  98  97  96  95  94      5  4  3  2  1

The Johns Hopkins University Press
2715 North Charles Street
Baltimore, Maryland 21218-4319
The Johns Hopkins Press Ltd., London

LIBRARY OF CONGRESS CATALOGING-IN-PUBLICATION DATA

Krieger, Murray, 1923–
    The institution of theory / Murray Krieger.
        p.        cm.
    A revised, expanded version of the lectures delivered at the
Academia Sinica, Taipei.
    Includes bibliographical references (p.) and index.
    ISBN 0-8018-4829-6 (hc : acid-free paper). — ISBN 0-8018-4830-X
(pbk. : acid-free paper)
    1. Criticism.   I. Title.
PN85.K65   1994
801′.95 — dc20                                          93-36343

A catalog record of this book is available from the British Library.

*For Joan, who shares my travels,*
*geographic and intellectual*

# Contents

# Preface

In May 1991, I delivered a set of three lectures at the Institute of American Culture (later renamed the Institute of European and American Studies) of the Academia Sinica, Taipei, Republic of China, Taiwan. I later converted my informal presentations into essay form for publication as a book by the institute for distribution in Taiwan. It bore the title *The Ideological Imperative: Repression and Resistance in Recent American Theory* (1993).

The invitation I originally received from the institute had asked me to speak on the rise of theory to institutional status in the United States, as well as the current state of that theory. Because so much of my career was dedicated to institutionalizing theory in the university, I had to acknowledge that my role in stimulating its rise made me an obvious candidate to undertake this report. In my lectures I tried to respond to what the invitation specified, tailoring my remarks to an audience from a distant culture, though one that had access to Western publications and was well informed.

My subsequent decision, made with the aid of good advice from the Johns Hopkins University Press and its editor-in-chief, Eric Halpern, to adapt these lectures into a book for a Western audience has led to significant transformations in the materials and the argument. I have thoroughly rewritten and expanded the three major chapters, inverting the order of two of them for the sake of what I now see as a developing, unified presentation; and I have added an epilogue, what I call a hortatory conclusion, to complete my summary of the paths that have led to the current state of theory as an institution, balancing our gains and losses in its attaining that state, and casting a wistful—I do not quite dare say hopeful—glance toward its future, while conceding the threats presently being leveled at theory's very authority to function.

Although I have made many changes and additions in bringing this volume across the Pacific, I have tried to preserve what I saw in Taipei as the general, that is, nontechnical, nature of its appeal. I must confess to enjoying the opportunity to indulge myself in these observations and their accompanying pronouncements about these past four decades, during which I have been an active participant in the growth of theory into a formidable institution, even perhaps in its decline during what may well be these post-theoretical days. In the past decade we have witnessed the polarization of almost all discourse concerning the humanities, as even moderate statements have been charged with being representatives of one extreme or the other. Despite this risk, I decided to add another more moderate voice, my own, in hopes of attracting a balanced, good-will response—one that would encourage the expansion of our range of texts and our ways of treating them, such as we have seen during the past two decades, while still recognizing and responding to the special powers of the literary text to help keep us and our culture—or should I not today say our cultures?—open to such an expansion of vision.

So I have tried to maintain the character of this treatise as a brief and direct statement, without burdening that statement with more than a few references to authors and works. There are of course many, probably too many, critical and theoretical movements that I have had to discuss or mention in passing. In order to distinguish their programs clearly for the reader as theoretical movements that have been accorded special names, I have consistently marked them by introducing each of their titles with a capital letter, even though in most instances doing so runs counter to the usual practice.

I have used rather interchangeably the terms or phrases *literature, poetic fiction, fictional text,* and *literary text* to signify what, following Aristotle, the history of literary criticism has termed *poetry*—of course, without restricting it to works written in verse. Indeed, I do not mean the reference of these terms to be restricted to any officially designated genres. Rather, I mean by them any text to which a reader attributes a fictional function, which a reader "intends" as a fiction in Aristotle's sense. This definition, generated out of reader reception, will include ostensibly nonfictional texts, as well as those that more obviously belong in it—although *any* of them may be read with or without being taken as "poetry."

I again thank the director and the staff of the Institute for European and American Studies in Taipei—especially Dr. Shan Te-hsing—as well as the receptive audiences they provided, for creating the occasion that sponsored the original lectures and encouraged their further development. And, as always, I am deeply grateful to my wife, Joan, who is my toughest and best audience.

*The Institution of Theory*

# 1  Institutionalizing Theory

*From Literary Criticism to Literary Theory
to Critical Theory*

IN EXAMINING THE PROCESS OF CREATING ACADEMIC INSTITU-
tions, I will be dealing with the relations between theoretical concepts and the development of operational university structures.
More bluntly, I will be exploring the intellectual accompani-
ments to, and the intellectual consequences of, academic politics. There is a politics at work, for better or for worse, in the
creation of institutions within the university; and the career of
important ideas is to a great extent dependent upon what the
institutional forces will permit. We have therefore in recent years
been witnessing in the United States an intense struggle among
a great variety of ideas to get footholds in those academic estab-
lishments that might permit them, first, to exist at all, even in a
minor way, and, as a next step, to foster institutional structures
that would be expected to encourage them to flourish. This continuing struggle creates an unusual situation in the history of the
academy in the United States, and I intend to pursue it in these
chapters.

When I delivered the original version of these observations
at the Institute of American Culture of the Academia Sinica in
Taipei, I could not help remarking that my host institute was a
general—by which I meant a multidisciplinary—organization.[1]
Such an interdisciplinary notion, still seen as somewhat revolutionary, would frighten, and has seriously begun to frighten,
those deeply entrenched elements that still are the principal
shapers of the humanistic institutions within the academy in the
United States.

That academy continues to trace its roots to the nineteenth-
century German model for organizing university structures,
based on careful distinctions among the disciplines. Still recog-

nizable in this conservative model is the conception of the so-called liberal arts inspired by Wilhelm von Humboldt, Prussian education minister and disciple of Immanuel Kant, who is to some degree the source of what we think of as the modern university, with its carefully demarcated divisions within the human sciences. In academic administrations and among many faculty in the United States, one can even now observe a steadfast attempt to hold onto the distinctness of the agreed-upon disciplines without seriously questioning their authority.

For example, one longstanding effort to loosen that rigidity was the development, some decades back, of what then were new interdisciplinary programs of comparative literature, which, after overcoming many attempts to discredit them, were finally admitted into the federation of disciplines we call the humanities. But this newly accredited hybrid, comparative literature, was, after all, only limitedly interdisciplinary, restricted as it was to literature, and to a few Western literatures at that. So, however hard comparative literature had to fight to gain general acceptance, it scarcely represented a radical concession to interdisciplinarity, at least as we look back upon it from our present institutional climate.

This traditional academic need for disciplinary security has not wanted its exclusionary definitions to be questioned, but assumes each of the disciplines has its own boundaries, which have been imposed upon them as if they were essential distinctions created by "nature" instead of by a limited philosophic line generated from the Aristotelian to the nineteenth-century German academy. Recent theoretical perspectives have reminded us that, as the development of too many societies has demonstrated, firm distinctions that have been confidently proclaimed as "natural" are later revealed as tremulous indeed, as no more than the projections of a very uncertain but power-driven set of human institutions that insist upon a certainty produced by ethnic and gendered and sociopolitical precommitments.

I want here to trace some of the history leading to the tensions within the American academy that I have begun to describe. Looked at from afar, some very strange things seem to have been going on recently: in some quarters a radical threatening of boundaries that seemed so solidly established, and in others a resistance, just as radical, against such threats. Institutional conflicts like these confuse us in other ways, too, as we seek to determine what they mean for the future of humanities and how they affect the recent ascendancy of theory as a shaping force within that future.

These recent developments may be viewed as having promising consequences for interdisciplinary and intercultural studies and thus for a newly broadened view of the humanities; yet they may also be viewed as having potentially destructive consequences for what we used to think of as the humanistic dimension of those same humanities. Further, these developments may be seen as resulting from the total triumph of the newest versions of literary and critical theory, while at the same time— and this, too, seems contradictory—they may also be seen as producing an end to theory, at least to theory as we have known it. This strange state of affairs, this set of recently visible contradictions, is not easy to straighten out, though I intend here to do what I can.

In the United States today it is difficult to recall that, not so many years ago—as late as just after World War II—in our universities neither literary theory nor even literary criticism was permitted to have a recognized role within either the literature or the broader humanities curriculum. For a variety of reasons, what was then called literary history—by which was meant the study of different historical periods and their total formative power to shape, first, literary "movements" and from them the interpretation of individual texts—was looked upon as the sole guardian over the discipline of literary study in any of the major Western literatures. I say it is hard to believe because today, within literature and the humanities, theory—as distinguished from, if not opposed to, history—has become not only an institution but also a potentially dominant institution, one that now threatens to reshape all the disciplines and indeed the very nature of what we think of the humanities themselves, though at the cost of, or perhaps with the express purpose of, driving literature itself (as we have known it) out of business. Strangely, this dominant role of theory persists even as theory itself has of late become threatened by the resurrection of history as a controlling force.

As one who some time back played a role in the systematic invasion of literature departments by theoretical concerns, I concede that I have a personal as well as a professional stake in this turnaround. More than once, people have approached me in recent years and said, in effect, "Look what you started! How do you like your monsters now?" And there are moments when I confess to feeling a bit like the sorcerer in *The Sorcerer's Apprentice,* who, as all the brooms come marching, no longer under any control and in numbers that can no longer be counted, wonders about what he has set in motion and what, consequently, has happened to the house that they were created in order to maintain. Yes, I concede that I was holding onto a fealty to the structure itself, though I wanted it to be commodious enough to contain elements that would subvert—though not quite deconstruct—it. This concession (or confession), I am aware, makes me an instrument of the power structure, which might well be using my aberrations to strengthen itself even as it admits and, indeed, encourages this liberality.

In the 1950s, when the New Criticism had not only invaded but begun to take over literature departments in the United States, universities had to come to terms with the general acknowledgment that we had entered what was called an "age of criticism." That phrase—and the word *criticism* here meant only literary criticism—was frequently used to describe what had taken place, just as today it is widely suggested that this is an age that is ending, or, more likely, that has already ended.

For many years—indeed, since at least the mid-nineteenth century—many of those speaking for American literature had been working to establish its own special character and its independence from the dominant literature in England or on the Continent. They wanted American literature to be viewed as nourished by its own specially American social roots in its own special ground. This desire was related to the myth about which much has been written—and which I will address at greater length in the next chapter—the myth of America as the New Jerusalem, the home of a collective American Adam, citizen of a new paradise, in its newness and innocence disconnected from the fallen Old World. What the dream of such a society required was the creation of an indigenous literature that would be true to this unique national destiny.

This kind of thinking was not altogether unlike some of what we hear today from those speaking on behalf of minority and Third World literatures. In the nineteenth-century United States it often led to a criticism that sought to separate what was happening, or should happen, in American literature from whatever had happened anywhere else. There was, then, to be no concern shown for the literary forms, conventions, or sources that had been controlling forces in the long existing tradition of literature in English that in imperialistic fashion would contaminate the literature of the New World. Rather, free of such hangovers, there was to be a continuing attempt to encourage and value only a literature that was responsive to the unique soil of this new, unique civilization. Such a mission meant a commitment to a sociohistorical criticism, which would treat literature as that which directly reflected the special properties of American life. The last thing it needed or wanted was any sort of aesthetic interest, and thus any sort of aesthetic criticism that suggested the refinements of another tradition, whether British or European. So, naturally, the emphasis was seen to fall on sociohistorical and cultural studies, concentrating on the environment as that which produced the character of the authors who produced the literary works.

This exclusive emphasis on historical context pretty well precluded an interest in any theory to guide the reading and interpretation of texts as specially literary, and hence aesthetic, "objects." Consequently most practitioners of what we now think of as the Old Historicism not only ignored theoretical concerns but also were irritated at any attempt to introduce them, little suspecting their own dependence on unquestioned assumptions that, grouped together, might properly be thought of as constituting *their* theory. And all I mean by "theory" here is the systematic rationalization of a set of guiding assumptions about the text and its relations to its author, its audience, and its culture at large.

As I insist in the next chapter, this was not the only kind of thinking, or criticism, that we find in the United States of the nineteenth or the earlier twentieth centuries. The aesthetic concerns of British and European traditions since the late eighteenth century also play a major role in the United States, but in the universities, at least through World War II, the historical concern with the social context of literature becomes an increasingly dominant force at the expense of the aesthetic. Ironically, this very tendency was only reinforced by its appeal to the tight philological disciplines disseminated by the German academic tradition as it applied "the higher criticism" to literary study. In this way European styles were indeed being invoked, though only because they could validate the native desire to permit Americans to argue for that kind of study which could reveal the special organic growth that their soil could alone cultivate. And the study of other literatures than their own was to be similarly dominated by concerns with biographical and more broadly historical contexts.

This situation in American departments of literature, in which the study of the special properties of the literary art as art, as literature, was de-emphasized, is what young scholars came upon when they returned from the war. Out of their frustration, their reaction against the lack of interest in the literary values of literature and, hence, in what later was referred to as "close reading," arose the rebellion that found its voice in an extra-academic movement, developing since the thirties, that came to be called the New Criticism and that, after the war, invaded and took over the teaching of literature in the universities. The focus now shifted to the literary art as consisting of a special collection of privileged pieces of discourse: all that had been bypassed, or even rejected, in the study of the peculiarly American character of American literature was now to be reasserted. It is well recognized that the New Criticism undermined the historical emphasis and instead sought to find formal and, more precisely, structural principles that could account for the special character of any literary work. Of course, this procedure would hardly single out American literature, but would treat any American text as just another contribution to a cosmopolitan Western tradition, subject to transcultural principles of analysis. The very source of this criticism came out of Europe: out of Russian and Czech Formalism and, earlier, out of the German organicism and the English romanticism that, in the United States, we have come to associate with the name of Coleridge.

The literary was to be a privileged mode of discourse calling for specially devised analytic techniques usable for no other kind of discourse. So the literary text was not to be studied for its relations to its origins. The politics of criticism had now turned from the attempt to relate the author to a rootedness in a personal and cultural environment or to any of the historical facts of the text's genesis, in order to concentrate on the formal internal interrelations that could account for the power of a literary work, *as* literary, to affect its audience. This way of reading the text could, in addition, help establish the claim for a theoretical structure of universal reading principles that might be then applied to other similar texts, thereby leading to a general theory of how to read all such texts.

Literary criticism was moving toward literary theory. It was moving from the study of a text to be read to a text that should be read closely and analytically to reveal its underlying structure and then, beyond, to reveal the relations between that structure and others in order for us to generate a theory of literary texts that could account for their literariness, that which makes them different from other, presumably nonliterary texts, with that difference to be pressed as strongly as possible. So criticism was to move from the single casual reading of any individual text to a criticism of that reading—that is, to the creation of a privileged or model reading, rationalized by a systematic notion of how such readings should be done—and from there to a formulation of that system; the formulation, in other words, of a literary theory that could account for such readings and in turn for texts being read in this manner.

In trying to describe the spirit of such criticism, at one time I described this tradition in literary theory as "words about words about words": theoretical words that were to account for the words of the critic that were to account for the words of the literary text itself.[2] The procedure moved from a given text to any random reading of it, to an authorized reading of it that was called criticism, and to the authorization for such readings that was called theory. It all used to seem quite simple and inevitable. This cultivation of a special aesthetic domain isolated literary texts from all other sorts of written texts, isolated literary study from the study performed by other reading disciplines, and thus isolated departments of literature from all the other departments within that collection of disciplines we call the humanities. Yet literature was also licensed to play a unique social role by being granted a special power, a way of functioning and of meaning unavailable to other kinds of texts, which enabled it in its own way to open a culture for its readers.

This was the beginning of literary theory as a professed academic discipline. That is, the New Critics wanted to read in a certain way, wanted to make texts valuable in a certain way, and in the course of doing so discovered that they were reading one text after another in certain authorized ways and that those ways were easily generalized into what passed for a literary theory. But theory as it was practiced by the New Critics had not yet been institutionalized; that is, theory was still not studied for its own sake. Theory, for the New Criticism, was at the service of the literary text; it existed only *for* the text. It was valued to the extent that it aided in the systematic exploration of that text, both in itself and in relation to its fellow texts. There was at that time a general agreement among the New Critics against treating literary theory as what T. S. Eliot called "an autotelic discipline," which functioned in order to serve only itself. On the contrary, it was insisted, the purpose of theory was *not* to be found within itself; instead, it was to *serve* criticism as criticism was to *serve* the canon of literary texts, and this service, presumably, was the justification for the interpretation of poetry as an academic activity.

So theory was looked upon as exclusively directed toward practice, toward the literary text—or, more candidly, toward a specified way of reading the literary text. There was to be no theory without immediate practical application, the practice of criticism. Theory required practical application; it was to function as an aid to systematically responsible reading. At the same time it must be conceded that the New Criticism justified what it was doing as having the large, democratic objective of improving the close-reading capacity, the critical-reading capacity, of an entire culture. You were to go to the university, learn the basic analytic methods, and proceed to read the great literary works of your culture in order to be a trained reading citizen, a citizen-reader. The justification of literary study and the reading discipline that defined it did not go beyond that social objective.

All theory, then, proceeded from a naïvely empirical assumption. The text was seen as an objective stimulus, loaded with structures waiting to be perceived and interpreted as such. That interpretation of the present text was similar in kind to others, and together they would constitute a system, a theory that would guide future readings. So one builds up from the particular to the universal, from the individual reading of a single text to the criticism that produces a rationalized or principled reading of that text—how we ought to read it to yield the best interpretive results—to a general theory that enunciates those principles so that we may go on to read other texts that have not yet been read for us this way. Theory was thus conceived as the systematic rationalization of the general presuppositions that underlie the reading of texts as literary texts. Theory begins and ends with those texts in their literary function and lives only for them.

Literary theory, thus defined and used, reinforces disciplinary distinctions and reinforces existing institutions without in any way moving toward creating a new institution for itself. It is not permitted to be freestanding, at least not in the late fifties and early sixties. Nevertheless, it would seem to be inevitable that, once this attitude toward literary texts flourished, the "age of criticism," as it was called, would gradually be transformed, even if against its will, into the "age of theory." That is where we have been for some time now, although that is not where critics writing in defense of theory thirty to forty years ago intended us to be. The impulse to theory, to generalization, and to the grouping of our experiences together in accordance with certain rational principles seems—from the commonsensical, empiricist perspective—to be an inevitable impulse. But once that theorizing impulse is let loose, it will, even if gradually, move toward shaking free of its dependence on experience in order to set up shop on its own.

This movement to set up theory as an independent discipline had its beginnings in the United States in the late 1960s, with the help, it must be conceded, of influences blowing across the Atlantic Ocean from France, first from what was called structuralism and later from poststructuralism. This is when theory could be

seen as breaking loose and developing itself as an independent
discipline—although, presumably, its function had previously
been to act only with respect to individual texts and to be justified only to the extent that it could help, through the criticism
it authorized, to illuminate them.

Once freed from that dependence on the readings of *literary*
texts, theory quickly and easily—at times far too easily—moved
into interdisciplinary mixtures within the humanities and, more
recently, even into the social sciences. Surely without meaning to
do so, the New Criticism had opened the door to the independent theorist, a theorist free of texts. Of course, to the extent that
it could be persuaded to admit theory at all—if only to justify its
own practices—the New Criticism was thinking exclusively of
*literary* theory, little believing that, once admitted, theory would
have its own imperialistic impetus and would spread beyond the
literary, indeed would subsume the literary. Once the New Criticism had sought to justify its interpretive practices, to generalize
those practices by enunciating a theory that called for them, that
theory was then out there in all its vulnerability, exposed to
the epistemological and semiotic critique that overtook it and
encouraged other and opposed theories to be promulgated. As
fashions changed, those challenging theories eventually won the
competition and in consequence broke through the isolation
that the New Criticism had imposed on literary texts and on literature departments alike.

During the years in which the dominance of the New Criticism went largely unchallenged, much internal pressure had
been building in reaction against the continual emphasis on the
closedness of the individual precious, incomparable literary work
that in its self-sufficiency too often seemed to speak to nothing
but itself. With the rejection of the New Criticism, newer theories forced literary texts to be opened up to the interests of discourse at large, in all its disciplinary variety, at once humanistic
and social-scientific. From that time many older as well as newly
developed disciplines have been rushing into the mix, leaving
us today with a confused arena of struggle among more wide-
ranging humanistic and social theories, but all of them displaying a radically interdisciplinary emphasis, which has completely

reversed the direction in which literary studies had been going and the way in which they would relate to the pursuit of what came to be called the "human sciences," a phrase that neatly joined the humanities and the social sciences.

The use of the phrase "human sciences" also indicated a shift in the domain of theory that turned out to be a major expansion of it. In assuming that theory, to the extent that it was permitted at all, was restricted to the domain of the literary, the New Critics could even authorize the phrase "critical theory" without conceding that they were moving beyond literature. For their willingness to countenance a "theory of literature" or "literary theory," which authorized them to read as they wished, could even be extended to a "theory of criticism" or "critical theory," which was used to validate the superiority of their theory over the others that had preceded theirs over the centuries.[3] They could not have expected that this latter phrase, with a different ideological history sponsored by its earlier use by the Frankfurt School, would serve the movement that would obliterate the "literary" in the interest of the an enlarged notion of the "critical."

For those later theorists who took up the Frankfurt School notion of the "critical" in "critical theory," the move beyond the New Criticism into the human sciences was accompanied by one principal motive from the time that their notion of theory was out there creating its own arena of debate. Once within that arena, it was inevitable that these newer theories—or newer versions of older theories—would seek to create their own institutionalized projections within the university; and that is what we have seen happening. Their one principal motive was the desire to tear away the privileged—indeed, the sacred—character of the literary, to "demystify" it (to use a favorite word), in order to argue, instead, for the primary force of the politically and historically contingent in both writer and reader.

There had indeed been something absolute and thus immutable in the assumed "objectivity" of the literary text as the New Critics instructed their students to read it, with its structures presumably out there waiting to be discovered. They thought it absolute in its power to override all contingencies: its meanings were universally present for any reader informed enough and astute enough to uncover them, in accordance with the stern commitment to the "disinterestedness" required by the post-Kantian aesthetic.

The reaction against such a conception by successors to the New Critics championed the return of the historically contingent and, consequently, the return of an interest in the social, economic, and political structures of value preferences that, at any moment in culture, condition how language works, how institutions work, how ideas are being developed and changed. All these create the text as a moving, changing entity, to be read differently at different times, to be conceived as having different meanings for the author as well as the reader from moment to moment. This is indeed the return of the text to the domain of contingency that controls all human activities alike. For well over a decade now critics have been concerned, not about the discovery of literary value, but rather about the socialized process of evaluation — the pressures to which it is responsive — in our different societies at different historical moments.

Consequently, we now must confront the argument that everything that earlier critics had claimed to find in texts, according to what their theories permitted them to interpret, they, like all readers, had themselves put into those texts. That argument runs counter to my earlier description of the empirical order, that naïve empirical sequence: the reading of the text, then criticism as the model or privileged way of reading the text, and finally theory as that structure of principles which would allow the authorization of such readings, moving from the particular to the universal. All those so-called objective claims that our infant theorizing had, in uncritical self-confidence, sought to justify were now to be deconstructed along with that theorizing itself, with the effect that the empirical order had to be inverted: the first shall be last. We were made aware of both critical and theoretical circularity in our arguments: the extent to which all the answers proposed by us as literary interpreters were predisposed by the way we framed our questions, which were largely determined by who and what and when we are, and, consequently, by what we, in advance, want and expect our answers to be. This predisposing is what I was assuming when I spoke of the inversion of the empirical sequence, because the so-called conclusion determines what we are looking for.

It is in this sense that what would-be empiricist criticism saw as the first now is seen as the last: the reading of the work is determined by the criticism, which is determined by the theory, rather than the other way around. And theory is itself determined by sociopolitical ideology. Thus, questions that turn out to be highly ideological will reveal in advance what, as interpreters, we have been seeking to find; and—lo and behold!—there it is, as we end up finding what we have been searching for; and we invariably do. We always manage to do so in how we read what we read. So our discourse is largely about itself; there may be no greater narcissism than in the delusion that we are seeking disinterestedly to learn about the discourse of another, only to learn that we have discovered the object that our own interests have led us to project.

In these newer theorists there is an acknowledgment, usually more elated than grudging, I fear, that there are no texts out there that are, properly speaking, primary texts, literary texts; no points of origin, when all texts, the poem and the commentary upon the poem, so-called literary and nonliterary texts alike, are similarly intertwined in the web of intertextuality, all controlled by the contingencies of the reader's preoccupations, primarily ideological, even if subliminally so. Consequently, if I may repeat the by now common argument, we do not first, as innocent readers, experience a text and then move to the interpretation of it and further to the general theory behind that reading, but instead we come loaded in advance with conscious or unconscious notions of what we are looking for, and then we manage to "discover" it.

Those notions serve as our theories, whether incipient or fully formulated, and are from the first in control of what we see and how we see it. The so-called empirical sequence that was to govern our *per*ception—from text to a reading of the text to criticism of the reading to the theory behind the criticism of the reading of the text—that empirical sequence is now seen as a *de*ception, produced by the need to gratify the controlling ideas in us that sponsor what we may think we are perceiving freely. Any theoretical structure comes to be exposed for what it is: a rationalization of our preferred way of seeing and judging, preferred for various reasons that have been impressed upon us by any one of the outside pressures that have shaped our seeing. Viewed this way, the entire aesthetic enterprise that was expressed by a text-centered approach like that of the New Criticism came to be reduced to nothing more than the prejudice of a leisure class, which would use this self-interested isolation of art to serve its own gendered, Eurocentric purposes.

In the universal skepticism for which such theorists argue, historical contingency is allowed to produce a theory that would undermine all theorizing except, of course, its own, because it would reduce all theories to their sociopolitical genesis sponsored by the dominant language of their culture, which governs them by means of its prior, subliminal, historically conditioned commitments. This is the primary thrust of various versions of New Historicist theory—whether in its Foucauldian, Marxist, Feminist, or minoritist forms—that have come along and completed the unseating of the New Criticism.[4] It is this radical historicist transformation that throws theory into business for itself, because it is the one theoretical thrust that would preclude all competition. Yet, by its very dedication to historical contingency, in the end it must argue against the need to theorize at all.

According to this recent thinking, several emphases, either singly or in combination, are required of us as interpreters if we are to understand the texts thrown up by the discourses of any culture: first, the primary role of the historically contingent, and second, the constant formative pressures of political power as expressive of class or ethnic or gender power—the power that would authorize the language generated by those whose interests we represent, in contrast to the language of those they would repress. These pressures shape the discourses of criticism and so-called literature alike. To these may be added the impositions of the psychoanalytical, of desire as socialized in discourse, which creates its own projections onto the language that both makes and controls culture. All these work to replace interpretation with a "hermeneutic of suspicion." Because no text is to be seen as innocent in its claim to mean what it says, one should read it only to search for clues to its subtextual agenda emanating from what Fredric Jameson has termed "the political unconscious."[5]

Consequently, this theory announces the end of any claim to value that is independent of party interest. We must remember that the establishment of value was a major element, if not the principal objective, of the New Critical reading. It was the intention of the New Critics to establish literary value, to establish a canon of literary works that were especially blessed with value — that *embodied* value — thanks to the verbal manipulations of their author. That is the quest for value that is now at an end; our most influential theorists now urge us, instead, to look into the sociological, psychological, and political processes that prompt the strange action we undertake when we evaluate. We are to study how and why we evaluate, rather than to determine what is worth valuing, what actually contains value, because evaluation merely reflects an imperialistic attempt to impose one's own prejudices upon others by claiming that the parochial values one supposedly discovers are universal, and universally available.

The circularity of the literary criticism and literary theory of high modernism, together with what is today charged with being its hidden political agenda, was thus unmasked. We came to realize that the confidence in the practice of previous literary criticism was, in circular fashion, backed by a theory that was developed solely in order to justify that criticism in its commitment to unlock for any reader the secrets of our most "valuable" literary texts (that is, those most responsive to, and hence "worthy" of, that criticism). This theory of literature, or literary theory, had easily slid into a theory of criticism, or what it called critical theory, to justify a dominant place for itself in the history of criticism and its theory. But it now was confronted, demystified, and overcome by a forcefully "critical theory" new style, which could override — by denying the force of — all literary criticism and the idea of the literary itself, which is to say, all literary theory.

Once the self-justifying notion of "critical theory" put forth by defenders of the New Criticism was replaced by a use of the phrase that had deconstructive force, it could not help reflecting also the earlier use of that phrase by the Frankfurt School to reflect the primacy of that school's political commitments. Looking well beyond the literary to *all* texts as similarly expressive of the sociopolitical (even if surreptitiously and thus subtextually so), and thus denying any distinction among kinds of texts that would privilege the literary, this postmodern theory was indeed critical of the claims for the transhistorical, uncontingent character of the theoretical impulse itself. In this sense, once it had done its work (in the interest of a single theoretical deconstruction of all other theoretical claims), this recent approach to critical theory, in being critical *of* theory, turned against the theoretical enterprise itself as necessarily metaphysical or, worse, essentialist in its appeal to transhistorical and uncontingent universals. Of course, it was implicitly excluding itself from these charges by denying any similar appeal to a grounding of its own claims. But this theory could proceed from such an exemption only while being insufficiently self-critical. Somewhere within its own principles of procedure and critique, but actively promulgating them, was a historically shaped political agenda serving as a universalizing subtext smuggled into the writings it controlled.

What motivates this radical shift to a theory that has been putting theory into a more and more powerful institutional place within American universities—even though, strangely, it happens to be a theory that denies both theory and the theoretical enterprise—is the larger movement in the humanities that has generically come to be called "antifoundationalism." This movement is perceived by our departments of philosophy, which seek to conserve the grounds of their traditional mission, as a threat from which they are in flight.

What is the foundation that this movement would question or, more devastatingly, deconstruct? What must be deconstructed, according to the early argument of Jacques Derrida, who is credited with being the father of Deconstruction, is the very foundation of Western philosophy: the logocentric assumption that behind our words and controlling their meanings are the independently existing concepts of "real" entities that those words seek to point us toward. This "reality" is the foundation, the ground, of our discourse. The foundationalism that authorizes our philosophical tradition springs from this uncritical logocentrism, this commitment to a "reality" that presumably precedes and directs discourse, a "reality" that constitutes a neutral realm of references, which transcends discourse and helps us judge any claim to "truth" that a piece of discourse might make. This neutral "reality" is to serve as arbiter in resolving competing claims about it made by competing discourses, each expressive of a partial and hence distorted perception. It is this set of epistemological assumptions that Deconstruction seeks to invalidate. To deconstruct that too easily assumed connection between the word and its stable referent is to pull down the foundation of Western philosophy.

This foundationalism, built into our philosophy since Plato, found in Immanuel Kant's monumental philosophical construct a fulfillment that could contain the modernism that followed. The post-Kantian construct rests on numerous assumptions, some of which I have anticipated: that there can be a "disinterested" pursuit of "truth" (if I may still use "disinterested," a word that is altogether rejected, and even resented, these days); that such a pursuit is very difficult, but theoretically possible, not to be ruled out in advance; that there is a neutral something out there, whether in the world or in the text—out there before any of us perceives it, something uncontingent—about which any dispute is at least potentially resolvable; in sum, that there is this foundation, this ground or origin, an ultimate point of reference behind each of our differing perceptions and our differing, or even our opposed, claims about it. Somehow, when all of our partial perceptions are subtracted from it, there is still some kind of "it" left, about which we can argue, which therefore constitutes a ground for debate. All these assumptions make up the meta-assumption of foundationalism, what many of the philosophies in the history of the Western world, philosophies long in disagreement with one another about most things, still would agree upon as the basis or ground—the stalwart foundation— for their debate. How can there still be a humanities or a notion of theory on the new grounds, or rather on the new groundlessness, of the antifoundationalism I have been tracing?

This radical epistemological skepticism (I hesitate to say "nihilism," as others too easily do) becomes dominant just at the time that theory *is* being institutionalized, largely because the antifoundationalist victory helps clear the way for that institutionalization. The way for theory has been cleared because texts themselves have been put "under erasure" (as it is said these days) by theory—even theory masquerading as history. There is, then, little to compete with theory, except perhaps history, which has been swallowed by theory. Or is it rather that theory is now being swallowed by history? If it is the latter, what is being promulgated is an *anti*theory theory. In the name of historical contingency, it rejects any theory that asks us to read and stay with the text instead of diving at once through it into a historically determined subtext. It rejects any theory that asks us to examine the validity of its statements as if they mean what they say within a system of meaning that stems out of the relationships of its parts to one another. We are rather to account for theory totally as an effect of historically contingent causes and the language constituted by them.

In view of the postmodern removal of the agency of the personal subject, it could be argued that there is no danger that this procedure can lead to the reduction that we used to call the "genetic fallacy" (literary critics, following W. K. Wimsatt and Monroe Beardsley, called it the "intentional fallacy"): those charged with it had presumably been guilty of reducing arguments to the motives apparent in the author's biography as a point of origin. This so-called fallacy was rejected long ago by the New Critics, but only in order to allow for the examination of verbal structures as if they were worthy of systematic analysis on their own. But, in flight from origins and trapped in the network of language, historicist theorists today, instead of treating individual author-subjects, treat "discourse formations" within language — these being driven by history's sociopolitical "realities" — as determining the subtext whose rhetorical power uses the text to sway the reader. I will consider in Chapter 2 whether one sort of genetic reduction has not been substituted for another.

To reject a priori the long-established methods of analyzing systematically what texts apparently (that is, as they come through surface analysis) intend to mean, as recent socio-historical-political commentators do, is to reject theory and the disciplined institutions that theory could traditionally authorize. As we have long known them, theories, as systems, have been the foundation of institutions; indeed, they themselves have become institutions. The antifoundational assault on theoretical constructs must be seen as an assault on institutions, although in the present case, however paradoxically, it is being conducted in order to replace one institution with another, an anti-institutional institution. Thus, strangely, the institutionalization of theory in the United States is most fully achieved when theory, except for its socio-historical-political reduction, is being deprived of its theoretical power.

What remains, a commitment to cultural theory (perhaps most forcefully represented in the movement called Cultural Materialism), seems hugely imperialistic in the hegemony it would extend to all the texts in a wide array of discourses—from traditional humanistic disciplines such as literature, philosophy, and history, to the law and a number of the newly softened social sciences, to the great variety of media we associate with popular culture and practices—all now run together under its aegis. This assault on academic structures of long and previously unquestioned standing would merge them into the single set of theoretical categories that would replace institutionally imposed disciplinary distinctions and dissolve their varied methods into a single set of reductive procedures.

Of course, there is no argument here that would claim a *substantive* unity among these disciplines; instead, the argument rests on a claim for the primacy of the principle of *difference,* which displays itself in the crucial verbal differences among classes, genders, ethnicities, sexual orientations. There appears to be an obvious contradiction in this attempt to elevate a single principle into an absolute, as if it were an essential methodological *and* substantive truth, even if—or especially if—it is a single principle intended to sponsor only endless differentiation. What we have, then, in this ultimate institutionalization of theory in the academy is a globalizing monolith of a theory, which gains ascendancy over the disciplines that it would transform in order to dissolve, in the process rejecting any less globalizing theories, which, locked within what had been firmly established disciplinary boundaries, had to be more modest in their claims.

Theory becomes institutionalized, then, at the expense of literature as an institution, at the expense of the literary as a privileged category, or indeed as any sort of a separate category to be distinguished from undifferentiated textuality. Early in my narrative I spoke of the conception of the literary text as a special kind of verbal structure, to be read closely for the intricacy of its internal relations that allowed it to become a mode of representation unlike that of any other kind of verbal structure—mainly because the literary text was not intent on doing anything but creating a self-involved fiction. But now we have seen that entire institution of literature dissolved and the literary text adrift with all others in a sea of textuality, or, to change to a currently more acceptable metaphor, interwoven with all other sorts of texts in the seamless web of textuality. A governing monolithic theory places these many varieties under the control of the sole agency of a sociopolitical subtext through which history's language speaks, usually repressively.

This egalitarian reduction of texts has stimulated—and has been used to justify—the recent mushrooming of humanities centers and institutes in our universities. Because this universal deconstruction has dissolved the boundaries among all the kinds of discourse and all the disciplines of the university, suddenly these radically interdisciplinary centers can begin to flourish. Such centers were a new sort of entity that seemed an appropriate companion to this recent foray into a theoretically inevitable multidisciplinarity—or, to put it more strongly, a theoretically inevitable move beyond disciplinarity altogether. Speaking as one who has created a major, well-funded institute and has helped to found an international consortium of such institutes, I can say with assurance that, as they address their ever-enlarging combinations of subjects, most of these are indeed institutes guided by theory, or even more by *a* theory, for the most part socially and politically defined.

Recently, when Ralph Cohen, the editor of *New Literary History* and founder of the Commonwealth Center for Literary and Cultural Change at the University of Virginia, and I, founder of the University of California Humanities Research Institute, were planning what we thought would be a small conference of the few people who were creating or had created humanities centers or institutes in universities around the country and abroad, we discovered that such centers had been cropping up everywhere. Indeed, we assembled what is probably a partial list of about one hundred fifty of them. Some were officially supported by their universities and thus were institutionalized, and some were self-selected groups of scholars of many disciplines who had gotten together on their own. Almost without exception, they were intended to function as anti-institutional growths within the academic establishment, collectives composed of individuals who, impatient with the inadequacy of what they felt to be the current state of the disciplines, were engaging in experimental intellectual collaboration in order to sew the varied discourses together.

Most such humanities centers have institutional ambitions. Even if they started as groups of intellectually disaffected individuals meeting informally, and even in a way subversively, their hope was to reach a size and quality that could allow them an intervention in the organization of their university in order, at the expense of the still reigning disciplines, to make it reflect their own theoretically sanctioned mission. Their pressure often led their administrations to give them the support that could lead toward institutional status. As they developed they served as what I have referred to elsewhere as "hidden universities." These were ad hoc enterprises of mutual instruction: beneath the recognized institutional structures and sanctions, without catalogue or curricula, faculty from widely disparate disciplines came together to educate one another and to subject themselves and their disciplines to the wider theoretical perspective that allowed them to become interwoven and thus to move beyond disciplinarity and its restraints. What was to emerge, first for the self-proclaimed center and then for the university structure it was to sponsor, was a reorganization of the way in which language and culture were to be studied and talked about. Some of this reorganization has occurred or is occurring in many institutions, with only a few that are total holdouts.

That much of this activity results from a healthy rethinking of unexamined or insufficiently examined academic dogmas is unquestionably true. The broadening of awareness in the human sciences and the loosening both of textual canons within disciplines and of disciplinary boundaries are producing new and salutary features in our universities, long in need of putting into question what had been held as sacred and thus as beyond question. They have also moved both philosophy and the social sciences as academic disciplines toward a new humanization, as well as bridging the often deep chasms that had developed between them and what we usually think of as the humanities.

It is also too frequently true that this new institutionalization of anti-institutional theory—as history tells us is so often the case—threatens to lead to new institutions as repressive in their own way as those they have sought to replace. Indeed, the rhetoric of these recent claimants speaks again and again of "the return of the repressed" or, worse yet, "the revenge of the repressed." Surely the latter only ensures a continuation of the sequence of repressions, and of the struggle for power that confers the power to repress with every momentary victory. Further and yet worse, this unfortunate sequence is pronounced inescapable, because everything rests on the theoretical insistence that there can be no outside appeal to any authority except that conferred by the force that comes with institutional power. Such are the consequences of pronouncing the total bankruptcy of any judgment that one claims is "disinterested," that is, not defined by an interest.

These consequences of antifoundationalism are indeed at a great distance from the high hopes of the modernist's claim for letters and for "high culture" (currently rejected as "elitist culture"). The modernist defenses of literature, and of art in general, we must remember, had insisted on privileging the arts because of their special powers, supposedly found within their complex structures, to contribute to our understanding of our human predicament as social creatures. Literary texts had thus been conceived as making their special contribution, beyond the power of other texts, because they could act as correctives to the monolithic, exclusionary directions that other texts, including theoretical ones, followed. As I argue in Chapter 3, they were to function as a culture's discursive resistance to the repressions of ideology.

Such a continuing oscillation of theoretical and ideological extremes as my narrative in this chapter has sought to recount seems to cry out for the hope of the balance of a *tertium quid,* some attempt at good will that, despite our limitations as "interested" creatures, would seek what Lionel Trilling had called a "liberal imagination." Whatever its weaknesses, the early commitment to theoretical enquiry, now almost half a century ago, had seemed dedicated to just such a liberality of imagination.

The sort of art and literature that had been highly valued showed itself—for the sake of broader human awareness—always sensitive to hearing the voice of the "other" as qualifying, if not undermining, what would otherwise have seemed to be the dominant voice of the text as an ideological instrument. And criticism and theory in those days tried to follow in the wake of such art and literature with a similar balance and sensitivity. Indeed, it was the restoration of this balance, producing a sensitivity to the value of the "other," that had been urged as a principal objective of the humanistic (hardly a popular term these days) as an enemy both to the repressive and to the repressive enemy of the repressive.

What was being urged was a renewed championing of the counterideological character of literature and, beyond literature, of literary criticism and a protective literary theory—in contrast to the recent transformation of *literary* theory into a more general *critical* theory. This interest in the counterideological, which has its own lengthy theoretical history, is the subject of Chapter 3.

## 2 Two Faces of an Old Argument

*Historicism versus Formalism in*
*American Criticism*

NOW THAT I HAVE TRACKED THE CAREER OF OUR THEORY AS
it has gradually become institutionalized, and before focusing
upon our current debates, I want to trace, within the history of
American culture, the roots of the opposition that have shaped,
and still shape, the issues that characterize those debates.

I use as my chapter title "Two Faces of an Old Argument" to
suggest certain parallels between the older debate that cast what
we now may call the Old Historicism against the New Criticism,
and the more recent and greatly transformed version of that
debate, which is quite strenuously current today in the United
States, that casts the New Historicism against Deconstruction.
At least I find certain important parallels, if not outright similarities, in the argumentative issues at stake in these debates despite
the major differences that must be acknowledged in the two sets
of antagonists. Of course, it is just as important to point out
these differences. A comparative examination of the two faces of
what I am calling an old argument should uncover, and perhaps
even clarify, a network of recurrent and illuminating problems in
theoretical disputation.

In what sense *is* the new version of the argument (if, as I say,
they are at root one argument) different from the old? Or do we
have little more than a repetition of the same argument in a new
and currently fashionable language? Are the antagonists in each
of the two opposed pairs within the debates — New Criticism /
Old Historicism, Deconstruction / New Historicism — more antagonistic to one another or more antagonistic to the analogue
that they are replacing as we move from one version of the argument to the next? In other words, how shall we relate the debate
between Deconstruction and the New Historicism to the debate

between Deconstruction and the New Criticism? Or, from the other side, is the major debate between the New Historicism and Deconstruction or between the New Historicism and the Old Historicism?

So there are several possible conflicts moving in these criss-crossing directions, all of them somehow to be implied by my title. It *is* an old argument, and it has had several different faces, two of them in the past half-century; and the extent to which we should be concerned with the difference in the faces *or* with the similarity within the argument is something I am at pains to determine.

Let me concede at once that my title is misleading: the argument is much older and wears many more faces than that title suggests, although I claim that the "two faces" are descended from that old argument as recent reflections of it, the first in the forties and fifties and the second in the seventies and eighties. But the shape of the argument goes back well before the New Criticism and its argument with the Old Historicism. It is, indeed, an archetypal argument within the entire history of American literature and culture as it is reflected in American criticism almost from the beginning. Throughout the nineteenth century there is a profound conflict about the basic idea of what an American culture ought to be, a conflict in curious ways foreshadowing the debates that are filling our discourse today. Indeed, we can go back even further and into a number of other cultural traditions to find similar debates in Western culture well before there was an American literature or an American criticism.

We can note, some time before the advent of an "American" culture, a somewhat similar conflict in the English literary tradition throughout the eighteenth century. It is not unlikely that this persistent conflict was transported to the United States to influence what happened here in the nineteenth century. I am speaking of what has been referred to as the conflict between Tory criticism and Whig criticism. It is immediately evident that these designations, being more political than literary, encourage our impression that the literary debate had its political source in the opposition between conservatives and liberals. We find a reflection of this conservative-liberal opposition in literary criticism in England, beginning with the late seventeenth century

and running through much of the eighteenth, in the much discussed "battle of the books," otherwise known as the battle between the ancients and the moderns, the battle waged about
both poetry (including prose fiction) and criticism.

Tory poets and critics (most often the same persons), tended
to insist upon current literature as no more than a modern adaptation, a responsible reflection, of longstanding literary traditions, or at least conventions, that could be traced back to canonical classical authors. It was understood that the ancients were
there to be copied and that the moderns, instead of arrogating to
themselves very much freedom to invent, were to emulate what
had already been well established from the classics onward in the
history of their literary tradition.

On the other side of the debate, the more liberal Whig tradition encouraged the freedom of poetic invention by a poet
licensed to look with his or her own eyes, unadulterated by a classical scholar's bookishness. It was the individualistic answer of
a literary Protestantism to the universalistic strictures of a literary Catholicism. Whiggish "dissidence" sponsored a private, self-
authorized vision that, unencumbered by previously authorized
ways of seeing and speaking, could yield an "enthusiasm" that
was as much a literary virtue for the critic as it was a religious
one for the Protestant cleric who passionately espoused it
throughout this period. In search of this subjective enthusiasm,
the poet was to settle upon being nothing less than an "original."
The notion of the original genius, projecting only his or her own
vision, as a representative of a singular moment in time and
space, arose to challenge the pallid work of the mere imitator.

Indeed, many aspects of the Tory-Whig opposition—in the
politics of religion and the politics of the state, as well as the
politics of literary criticism—were reflected in the battle of the
books. Behind that opposition and affecting every manifestation
of it were two opposed myths, which projected different narra-
tives of human history from the beginning. The first of these is
the myth of a prelapsarian golden age, followed by the decline of
human society. The original canonical poets, Homer and his
equally classical follower Virgil, were the golden poets, and because, from that time the world, guided by the spirit of entropy,
has pretty well run downhill, we would do best to follow them

rather than to trust to ourselves. This myth of cultural history is obviously related to its religious companion, the myth of the Fall of Man, which calls for traditional churchly guidance much as the modern poet requires classical guidance. The role of this thinking as support for a conservative theory of literature should be evident enough.

If in their fallen days eighteenth-century writers could only hope, however futilely, to emulate the golden age, they might well call the English neoclassical age the Augustan age, with King George II as the worshipped parody of the imperial greatness of the original Augustus, and with Alexander Pope, reborn imperial poet, writing "imitations" of Horace and both translations and parodies of Virgil. The severe differences in the times, the societies, and the cultures between the two Augustan ages, the classical and the neoclassical, might mildly modify, but were not to obliterate, the severe authority of the sublime first over the inferior second. Here indeed was the conservative claim for an atemporal universality of form and value.

The second and opposed myth was the myth of progress, whose narrative of human history took as inevitably upward a direction as the first took a downward. Born out of the rationalist dreams of the Royal Society, nurse to an emerging scientific utopia, the idea of progress justified hopes for a world that would continually improve because it would be guided by the moderns of any period, who had the benefit of knowing more than those who had gone before. So, in contrast to the downward movement from an original golden perfection, culture is to move from ignorance toward the perfection that its ever-increasing knowledge will make possible. Similarly, the modern writer, with superior knowledge, would surely go beyond all those who, in greater ignorance, came before. Clearly, then, the modern must not be constrained by any of those earlier writings that an educated superiority is committed to surpass. Each generation must write a new literature for itself, a literature responsive to the peculiar needs that give rise to it.

A consequence of this second view was to encourage a literature that, far from being universal, above history and the changing contexts that history provides, was primarily attentive to the special character of the cultural moment in history that surrounds and sustains the writer. This freeing of the poet from what seemed like artificial classical attachments is what, more than a century earlier, Edmund Spenser's poet-speaker called for in *The Shepherd's Calendar* (1579). At the outset of his career, though he is writing in an apparently classical form, the pastoral, with the many necessary classical borrowings that come with it, and though he even refers to the poet-shepherd's model poet by using the Latin version of his name, Spenser is nevertheless fighting for his special native voice in defiance of the obvious classical models.

To turn his pastoral into a poem that speaks the plain language of the people instead of the elegance of classical learning, Spenser's poet turns against the very classical poet who is his source for the pastoral. Speaking for "the new poet" (Spenser), the apologetic author of the poem's extended dedicatory preface, "E. K.," announces Spenser's explicit rejection of "the Roman Tityrus Virgil" in favor of the more recent English "Tityrus," Chaucer, the "good old poet," whom "the new poet" treats as the great originator of the English poetic tradition, together with the language necessary to it. Treating "the new poet" as an experimental poet trying to create a vernacular, E. K. justifies Spenser's turning from "the sound of those ancient poets" to "old and obsolete words [as] are most used of country folk." Their "rough sound would make his rhymes more ragged and rustical" and thus are "fittest for such rustical rudeness of shepherds."

Spenser's poet-speaker himself tells us (in the June eclogue) that he does not "presume to Parnasse hill," but instead is "piping low in shade of lowly grove," using a "homely shepherd's quill." Claiming fidelity to Tityrus (the English Tityrus, Chaucer, rather than the Roman Tityrus, Virgil) as the only "god of shepherds," he acknowledges that it is most appropriate for him to sing in "rhymes" both "rough and rudely dressed." *The Shepherd's Calendar* is in many places a dark pastoral, with Spenser's peasant-shepherds often undergoing bitterly realistic suffering from their labors in the raw northern climate, indeed at a great distance from their southern, sunny, mythic forebears in Theocritus. Further, several of the eclogues in *The Shepherd's Calendar* are written in what Spenser conceives as the crude native English verse forms and archaic diction of the Middle Ages, in contrast to the classical regularity that comes to England through Italian poetic conventions.

Indeed, a general study of late sixteenth-century English poetry reveals the conflict between the conventional allegiance to, and borrowings from, the Italianate version of the classical tradition and the attempt to create a homely but energetic, purely English poetry springing out of native soil. This conflict was part of the wider struggle, manifested in activities as distant from each other as fashion and religious politics, concerning England's insular role in the wider world of the Renaissance, the latter represented by the despised Italianate Englishman in fashion and art, and in religion by the Roman Catholic church as opposed to the recently founded Church of England. All are manifestations of a national culture, which sees itself as young and vigorous, and which seeks to find its own literary voice in *its* language, without adapting it to the preestablished harmonies of older and elegant, but wearied, voices of the past and of those effete cultures bound to the past.

Spenser's quarrel with the universal, classically justified language of the dominant Renaissance style in order to create a native literary language, and thus a truly native literature, is an echo of Dante's quarrel, several centuries earlier, with the insistence that his epic, as an imitation of the classical epic, should be written in Latin rather than in the modern language of his own national culture. Dante justified the force of his native Italian as the language of the *Commedia* in his treatise that argued for his use of the "vulgar" rather than the classical tongue, making the claim for a "vulgar eloquence." He was creating the model for a new national literature as well as for a literature that has moved beyond the break between the medieval and modern worlds. This cultivation of the "vulgar" became the precedent for those several later moments, like Spenser's, in which poets seek to represent changes inevitably wrought by history's movements through the evolution of cultures and the creation of new ones.

It was precisely this attempt to create a radically new culture that inspired the defenders of a uniquely *American* literature, one that, in its self-assertion, was to be cut off from its mother country and from Europe in general. As I have suggested with my examples from Dante and Spenser, any new literature, representing a culture that is striving to create its own identity, seeks to create a literature in its own language as a way of opening its culture to a new vision, in the process freeing itself from the controls and limitations of the old language of its ancestors. Nowhere was this effort stronger than with those dedicated to a literature for the New World, indeed the New Jerusalem, that they saw in the United States. In Chapter 1 I referred to the Edenic myth—proposing an "American Adam"—that sponsored the dream of a uniquely American literature that was to be as severed from the English and broader European establishment as was the nation itself, conceived on a new ground as a new chance for humankind, as if free from the Fall, to start again.

Those holding this progressive dream were deeply disturbed by the extent to which the Old World was keeping its hands on that new literature, stifling it, preventing it from speaking in its own special, prelapsarian voice. But for a long time—well into the nineteenth century—most of our leading literary figures were on the other side, asking the raw writers of this primitive land to produce "civilized" work, to learn and adapt to the exemplary refinements that English and European writers and critics had made available to them. They saw American culture, at its best, as an imitative spin-off from England as the mother country. Indeed, for much of the nineteenth century, despite some strong voices raised in native opposition, the dominant argument of the American literary "establishment" called for American literature to serve as a branch of English literature.

There was, then, a crucial ideological conflict between those seeking a truly American literature, reflective of the New World, and those seeking a cultivated transplanting of English literature that would be an extension of it. Ironically, far from being unique to the United States, the conflict is as common as it is inevitable for any young culture seeking to establish an independent voice. The American version of this conflict has had important theoretical consequences for American criticism that extend to our own day.

Feeding the conflict was one additional incentive for creating a radically independent American literature: its need to reject an aristocratic, Old World elegance, in order to be expressive of a radical experiment in democracy—the world's first—and the unique culture that such an experiment can produce. So, it is argued, the new American culture is not simply making the same claim that other new cultures make, but, because it is something special, it has a claim to uniqueness unknown heretofore.[1] It is creating a new paradise for the commom man, granting him an unprecedented freedom. This theme runs through those in the American nineteenth century who are arguing for a new literature that reflects the wilderness, the frontier, and even the Native American cultures, and that turns its back on the cultures that are inherited from the Old World and that necessarily reflect its politics.

The urgency of the movement toward American independence, in art as earlier in politics, may have made the defense of Old World literary habits more difficult, but the desire for a genteel culture for the New World's elite prompted many of our most established writers to undertake such a defense. They argued that the objective of American culture should be to show how quickly and thoroughly it could demonstrate the growth of its "civilized" character, of its own elite, worthy of joining the world's best, rather than to urge the rough commonness of a new barbarism.

More than half a century ago the two opposed tendencies that fought this conflict were most helpfully, if reductively, characterized in a very small but very influential article by the American critic Philip Rahv, with the simple but telling title "Paleface and Redskin."[2] Borrowing racist terms from an earlier era, Rahv means to polarize two tendencies, the effete European and the robust Native American. His was surely too simple a dichotomy because there are relatively few unqualified examples of one or the other. Most writers mix these extremes, but since they are likely to tend more in one direction than in the other, there may be some advantage in using Rahv's terms to identify the polar reach of either side. Rahv saw the "paleface" as the defender of English or European elegance and refinement, while he saw the "redskin" as the defender of Native America in the raw: the "decadent" on one side and the "primitive" on the other.[3]

The most influential "palefaces" were found among the literary leaders of the mid nineteenth century, and for some time their program was kept in force with little serious challenge by the "redskins." We identify these leaders primarily with New England, indeed with Cambridge, and, most narrowly of all, with Harvard University. The names of three so-called Brahmin stalwarts, James Russell Lowell, Oliver Wendell Holmes, and Henry Wadsworth Longfellow, furnish examples enough. Each of them is a Massachusetts writer with strong ties to the literature of the Old World; each is anxious to promulgate an American version of English literature, a version that will be justified only to the extent that one day it will be able to stand competitively with its parent literature.

The "redskins," on the other hand, were rugged defenders of the frontier, who wanted to respond to the new dispensation given humankind to create the "American Adam," to live in a new Garden of Eden, as if before the Fall. Here is a creature destined for progress, even perfection; certainly a creature free of the fallen world of Europe and England, the world that had fallen into moral and aesthetic bankruptcy and that, from the standpoint of the American, forced the people who became the United States to flee there from Europe and to create their radically new society. What was called for in the United States was a literature that was fit companion to that new society. Although this was a muffled voice for much of the nineteenth century, in the later decades of that century it emerged more and more forcefully.

This conflict, strongly evident by the later nineteenth century, continues into much of the twentieth. Many critics have spent an enormous amount of energy arguing whether and how there can be an American literature. However, the early writers we used to think of as the important writers in the United States, those who quickly won their place in the canon of nineteenth-century American literature, are for the most part associated with the Old World.

Even a writer such as James Fenimore Cooper, who from the 1820s writes about Americans committed to the westward movement of the frontier—about Leatherstocking—is, strangely, writing literature that is less "redskin" than "paleface" (if I may continue to use this admittedly oversimplified opposition). Despite his subject, Cooper remains faithful to European notions and even, in a foreshadowing of Henry James and others, takes up an extended residence in Europe. He is an unhappy aristocrat in temperament, uncomfortable in the New World, which is his own world, even as he writes about it. His very Native Americans, as well as his American heroes, have something of the elegant European about them and, as might be expected, appeal to European as much as to American audiences. There is thus a conflict, indeed a contradiction, between Cooper's subject, which frequently is the New World frontier, and his treatment, which is that of a would-be European seeking to assimilate the newest of the New World to the customs and the morals — and even to the speech — of the Old World that he admires. Indeed, besides his relatively few frontier romances, which in many ways resemble the historical romances of Sir Walter Scott, Cooper writes many other works that are openly European in subject as well as attitude.

Other European-style American authors through much of the nineteenth century show even less uncertainty in serving their cosmopolitan tastes. The so-called Brahmins of Cambridge, of Harvard, to whom I have referred, acknowledge and would extend the influence of European masters: by translation, by allusion, or by discipleship in ideas, style, and form, one or another of them invokes Dante, Goethe, Coleridge, and others. Indeed, through Lowell, for example, Coleridgean criticism — the English version of German theories — is introduced to guide and judge American literary development.

There are other, though more complex and mixed, voices. For example, Ralph Waldo Emerson is responsive to major European ideas, including those of Coleridge, but he joins them to deeply native commitments. Thus his work is compounded of both sides of the conflict between the American and the European in its effort to find the special combination of learning and spirit that constitutes what he calls "the American scholar." Although borrowing many of the theories of his European masters, he calls for a robust, open-ended American individualism, a freedom from historical conformity, in his argument *against* domination by the European influence.

We can also observe this conflict in the unending quest to find "the great American novel," as well as in the equally extended argument about what this phrasing of the quest means.

There is an unquestioned breakthrough of a special American voice in fiction, and an internationally influential one, in the work of Nathaniel Hawthorne and Herman Melville, though both of them have their links to English, if not generally European, traditions. In later nineteenth-century fiction we can also point to the contrast between William Dean Howells, whose modest novels are an optimistic celebration of small-town America, and Henry James, the anglicized American, whose elegantly refined novels celebrate a Continental vision and a meticulous cultivation of form that allow them to claim a place of special eminence among late nineteenth- and early twentieth-century English novels. Indeed, James foreshadows what T. S. Eliot, the anglicized Saint Louis American, does to English (and American) poetry a couple of decades later.

Whatever arguments there may be about "the great American novel," there is little question that Walt Whitman in the later nineteenth century claims the role of the supremely American poet. His poems, having been persistently liberated from what had been accepted verse forms, celebrate the rugged egalitarianism, the honest crudeness, the new sensibility, of the American experience. In prose, from his 1855 "Preface" to *Leaves of Grass* to his *Democratic Vistas,* Whitman calls for a vision for this new culture, whose open individualism and optimism, whose social vision, are to be directly reflected in a literature that has turned its back on the tired conventions of an aging Europe. Out of the vision of Whitman, and in part Emerson before him, comes a series of poets and critics well into the twentieth century who are similarly devoted the new version of humanity, and its appropriate literary forms, that American soil can breed and nurture. But as I have already anticipated in my glance forward to Eliot, the cosmopolitan perspective has hardly left the field.

What we may view as a conflict among poets and novelists is intertwined with the conflict among critics. The examples I have been citing throughout America's literary history, and many others we could observe, demonstrate the continuing opposition between the attempt to merge American literature into a long, cosmopolitan literary tradition and the attempt to create a radically new literature for an infant culture, one severed from the European tradition that would claim its rights to parentage. We can, for example, observe an early twentieth-century version of this critical conflict in the work of James Hunecker, an American version of the European fin-de-siècle aesthete, on the one side, and on the other Van Wyck Brooks, a celebrant of the native tradition, who clearly announces his position with the title of his early book *America's Coming of Age*. And so it goes, even to the present, with whatever incidental changes.

The oppositions that I have delineated — admittedly with strokes that are much too broad — and whose histories I have been rapidly tracing have all been incipient forms of the "old argument" of my chapter's title. Each of these visions calls for its own theory of what literature is and how criticism ought to treat it, a theory quite at odds with the alternative theory.

The attempt to put American literature into the lengthy Western tradition of literary conventions of form and genre leads to a criticism that is essentially aesthetic, even formalistic. It should, that is, concern itself with the extent to which these new literary texts written by Americans are better or worse examples — more or less developed examples — of the standards set by the writings we have had before us in the great literatures of the West. Let us put the Americans into a competition with what has been produced by the rest of Western culture, and let us use similar criteria to see how they measure up, on the same terms. And let American authors learn all they can of past literatures in order to match or exceed them, but according to standards derived from them. These directives call for a criticism that is essentially formalistic, treating literary texts with universal criteria and seeing them as containing certain values, so that they open themselves, regardless of time and place, to prescribed ways of being read and placed.

On the other side we have a profoundly different view. We are to judge American literature by the extent to which it is shaped by and directly reflects American experience, this special kind of experience that only this land could yield.[4] In this case, literature is to be read as an utterance of its unique cultural context, as a direct reflection of its surrounding social reality. It is a growth that only *its* soil can produce. It cannot help, then, but be an instrument of ideology, even if the idea of the United States is supposed to guarantee that it is a perfected ideology of "freedom." Only the United States or, rather, the myth of the United States, can press its ideology without doing oppressive harm. Here is the precedent for later ideological theorists who, by claiming the privilege of freedom for their own ideology, can exempt it from their concern with ideological repression everywhere else.

The theory of historicist reduction, though strongly influenced by the growth of the desire for a distinctly American literary voice, was reinforced, at least in the American university, by the theoretical claims behind the European philological tradition that helped formulate the program of American academic research in literature. From its early days in the nineteenth century, European positivism sought to turn literary study into a science seeking verifiable knowledge about the environmental circumstances behind literary production. Its positivistic restraints led it to distrust the unverifiable impressions of literary critics. "History is objective; criticism is subjective": this is the way an old professor of mine, a distinguished historical scholar, used to conclude authoritatively in order to repress our literary enthusiasms. Although this attitude in the American academy was, ironically enough, a borrowing from Europe, it was the one borrowing that the programmatic Americanist happily made, because there was such a coincidence of objective in positivist and Americanist theories about the relations of literary works to their sociohistorical genesis.

It is this reduction of the literary work to its social, and hence ideological, context that leads to the traditional modes of academic historical research that we now think of as the Old Historicism, which studied the work exclusively as a product and reflection of the social "reality" that surrounds it. There was in it an assumption of a one-to-one relationship between verifiable elements we can identify in historical documents and elements in the literary work. On the other side of the argument by the 1940s was the New Criticism, which concentrated its interest on the literary form exhibited by the work before it. It sought to read the text—any text, regardless of time and place—exclusively within that text's own constellations of internal relations.

The New Criticism was inherited from the work of Coleridge, who was a major influence on Lowell, chief among those

I have treated as major nineteenth-century representatives of American criticism in the European style. So the lineage—and it also runs through James and Eliot—is continuous. And so is the argument, as well as the lineage, of the opposing side. The conflict in the nineteenth century can be viewed as the "Lowell side" against the "Whitman side." Descended from Whitman, the Old Historicism (at least among scholars in American literature) insists on relating every literary work to the soil out of which it alone could, and must inevitably, grow.

By the time we reached the forties, just before and after World War II, the conflict between the Old Historicism and the New Criticism became quite intense. This early conflict, which was also a fight to control the mission of university literature departments, is traced in Chapter 1. I could cite many examples of severe quarrels, both about specific texts and about general critical principles, from that moment.

On the one side, the New Critics charged that the historicists, concerned only with the surrounding society and its influence on literary works, were absolutely tone-deaf, without sensibility, unable to respond to what a literary work was capable of performing as a literary work. On the other side, the historicists (still Old Historicists) accused the New Critics of scholarly ignorance, of having none of the historical knowledge of the ideas and ideologies, the allusions and references, that together could account totally for the meaning of the literary work under consideration.

As in most polemical disputes, as we look at them now from this distance of time, the two extremes of the Old Historicist-New Critic debate may seem a bit absurd in the extremity of the charges on both sides. How can either side have been altogether guilty of its opponent's charge? Any literary text consists of language; and how can any language function without its being informed by the historical moment in culture that creates it? Surely no commentator trying to be responsive to the language of a text could help but be attentive to the need for the requisite historical knowledge. But we can ask from the other side, how can a commentator, no matter how thoroughly armed historically, read complex texts without being aware of the need to read them intensely *as* texts, in large part by searching for the internal relationships among the words and groups of words that make the text what it uniquely is? It was no more likely that a New Critic was thoroughly ignorant than it was that an Old Historicist was thoroughly insensitive to literary values.

And yet the old argument between those primarily dedicated to a text's historical relations and those primarily devoted to intratextual readings *has* continued and, apparently, *will* continue, though under a variety of faces. One of the main reasons for the argument persisting as it has is the theoretical one I have suggested in my survey of American attitudes toward the nature and function of literature: the continuing opposition between those who would account for the literary work as an immediate reflection of its contemporary culture and those who would put the literary work in competition with all others by relating it to transhistorical formal standards based on reading and evaluating procedures that are treated as being universal rather than culture-bound. For the one side literature is one of the many inevitable, totally determined, manifestations of cultural, mainly sociopolitical, forces, so that a study of cultural history shows us what the related literature shall—nay, must—be. The other side sees literature as an independent institution with its own history, with each new text entering the realm of value established by its forebears, as it seeks to transform and exceed them.

This latter alternative has surely been altered profoundly these past two decades in the hands of Deconstruction, which refuses to isolate and thus privilege purely *literary* texts. But if, instead of the reading of literary texts, we substitute the "reading" of any one of a variety of kinds of texts—a reading that has much in common with the practices of what with the New Criticism was the art of reading literary texts—then the structure of the argument may not be very different after all. What we used to think of as the literary is, according to Deconstructionists, to be expanded to the entire realm of textuality, all of it now treated as one tropological and narratological verbal sequence. This theoretical shift carries us into the final (until now) version of our longstanding argument.

In more recent years we have seen the old argument take on the new face that reflects the debate between Deconstruction and the New Historicism. If we are to understand the differences between the two faces, we must first make clear in what way the New Historicism is different from the Old and in what way Deconstruction is different from the New Criticism. One cannot begin to answer these questions without recognizing the extent to which, however great their differences from each other, the New Historicism and Deconstruction have something in common against both the Old Historicism and the New Criticism, the earlier pair of antagonists.

With its prestructuralist assumptions, the Old Historicism assumed that, since history was a series of facts solidly out there, objective and verifiable, it was itself in no need of being interpreted. In other words, history was not problematic. By contrast, literary texts were problematic and thus in need of being interpreted. We were to use the known to interpret the not yet fully known: we were to use history to interpret texts, to use history's "facts" to resolve problems of interpretation found in texts. It was a reaffirmation of the old distinction — as old as Aristotle — between history as real and texts as imaginative fictions. Such were the consequences of the naïvely positivistic conception by the Old Historicism of history as facts rather than history as discourse.

About twenty years ago, with the advent of poststructuralism, history, like all other forms of discourse, was put into question. What if history was not merely a collection of external, "objective" facts? After all, was not history, as a form of discourse, written as a narrative and, as such, already an interpretation of so-called facts? So history itself came to be regarded as problematic, no less so than any other discourse, only perhaps more deceptively so, because it usually appears (pretends?) to be a factual report. History, then, is itself a text in need of interpretation and has no privileged relation to "reality" that would permit it to be used to interpret other, less "real" texts. So goes the poststructuralist argument about the textual character of history.[5]

So history is no longer, as it was for the Old Historicism, simply *there,* as a series of documents recording a fixed sequence of facts — of unquestionable knowledge — that, once established by the scholar, could be used to try to make sense out of the more troublesome literary text. Poststructuralism and its historical agent, the New Historicism, have taught us that we get those claimed facts out of books, which are also interpretations and have their own narratological and tropological structures, have their own reasons for being written as they are: whether or not we like it, they in turn stand in need of also being interpreted. Indeed, the historical text may well take no less interpretation in the reading than does the literary.

This was the consequence of the one major claim of post-structuralism in all its varieties: that reading any sort of text does not lead us to dispute about realities and unrealities in the world. It is, instead, a matter of looking at the entire world of would-be knowledge as a world of language, a world of discourse or, better yet, of textuality. In light of such a shift, the New Historicist discovers that the primary assumption made by the Old Historicists can no longer be made: we can no longer look at a given moment in the history of culture as if it is out there to be known directly, independently of language, as a collection of brute realities, which we can simply apply to literature in order to reduce the more resistant literary text to its place in its cultural moment.

Instead of this simpler assumption, we now are to assume that the reader who would relate all sorts of texts to one another is like a juggler who has a number of balls all moving about in the air at the same time. One of them may be literature, one may be history or any text in another discipline within the "human sciences," and no one of them is, a priori, any more stable than any other. All texts are to be read similarly, as equally unstable bits of language requiring interpretation, with no one of them a fixed instrument to be used to unlock any other. So, once again, history can reveal no self-evident facts that allow it to be an interpretive agency for the uncertainties of the literary text. It follows also that literature should not be treated as a mode of discourse different from history or any other mode of discourse, since all share a similar problematic of representation. Current methods of interpretation, consequently, tend to take what used to be techniques employed exclusively for reading literature and to impose them upon a variety of textual kinds, all now made equally responsive to such readings.

A commentator who seeks to be historical now must look at a variety of kinds of contemporaneous texts and relate them to one another by finding common elements among them—meta-

phors, narrative structures, in short, Foucault's "discourse formations." The New Historicist, then, allows these texts from
many domains to read one another, treating them all as parts of
a single discursive moment in culture, as flowing into one another in what a founder of the New Historicism, Stephen Greenblatt—in a metaphor borrowed from biology—calls a "circulatory system."[6]

Having canvassed the texts of a given cultural moment in
order to discover a common discourse formation, New Historicists do not stop there in their historical concern. They must
eventually reach beyond discourse to uncover the sociopolitical
forces that create the peculiarities of its formation at the moment
in question. The particular discourse formation, seen displaying
itself in its various textual manifestations, reveals common narratological and tropological structures, which function rhetori-
cally to prejudice judgment, elevating or at least protecting some
elements in society by repressing others. It reveals certain hierarchies of power, of repressor and repressed, within the social
fabric of that moment, those hierarchies—of race, class, gender—that create its discourse. Who is wielding the power and
over whom? Who is being denied the power, and with what
costs? How are the limits of discourse being defined and imposed? And whose interests are being served? It is not surprising
that such questions lead historicism in a sharply political direction in response to pressures from marginal voices, long repressed, to alter the ruling discourse formation in order to impose their own, even if no less repressively.[7]

Within its historical moment, then, every ideology is seen
as creating its language, and through that language speaking
each variety of discourse, lying in wait under the text to capture
the reader. New Historicist theory, whether supporting Cultural
Materialist or Neo-Marxist or Feminist or minoritist or Gay
and Lesbian critics, can alert us to the single subtext—driven by
power—that each would find beneath all contemporary texts,
and by means of that subtext warn us of the political mischief it
would work upon the unwary reader. So New Historicists must
finally be concerned about the actual power relations within a
society, even though, as poststructuralists, they derive all their
definitions of power from a reading of the way in which the var-

ied texts of a given period, through mutual reflection, can be seen as controlling and speaking the language of the power they represent.

Because, as American critics have used it, the language-centered episteme they take from Foucault is empowered by the sociopolitical context, the New Historicists' claim may in the end turn out to be not altogether unrelated to the claims of the Old Historicists, who were echoing the earliest defenses of an American literature emerging out of the American grain. In this one sense, then, the New Historicism might be seen as at least an inheritor of the Old Historicism, if not an extension of it. In another sense, of course, its entire procedure means to be different, thanks to its theoretical need to merge historicism with the poststructuralist commitment to the special role of discourse.

Consequently, the New Historicist faces a methodological, and ultimately a theoretical, dilemma: how to claim, as a poststructuralist, the primacy of a dispersed textuality and yet to claim, as a historicist, the primacy of brute power relations in a social reality. However much these relations may be constituted by the culture's discourse, at some point they come to be directed by forces that are outside language and hence that serve as a forbidden "myth of origin" for them. This dilemma is, for New Historicists, an insoluble chicken-and-egg problem, because priority becomes impossible to assign without forfeiting one half of the double claim of priority that they must make—a claim on behalf of both history and textuality. And their political program prevents them from saying, in the spirit of poststructuralism, that history and textuality are one.

By contrast, as the latest version of "paleface" commentary, American Deconstruction, dependent on Continental sources, is in some strange way playing the cosmopolitan role of defending close textual reading that was played earlier by the New Criticism, even though Deconstruction attained its recent dominance in the American academy out of its strenuous opposition to the New Criticism. The Deconstructionist rejects the New Criticism for insisting on the specialness of poetic discourse, but, even more, for insisting that this specialness was defined by a miraculous formal presence of meaning constructed into a closed system. To the contrary, the Deconstructionist, as a poststructuralist, finds all texts, poetic or otherwise, similarly opening onto the expanding series of verbal sequences, all of them filled with "traces," the ghosts of language past. Hence they are open to being seen as referring to one another within an endless regression that constitutes the retreating, yet always echoing, realm of textuality. Indeed, there seems to be no way for the mutuality of textual meanings within this series to reach beyond the parade of signs to any "reality" except one that can be conceived in a discursive form.

Within the realm of human discourse, the world is subsumed by the complex network of the intertwined language of our texts, despite our retrograde logocentricity, the mystified belief that we are talking about the "real thing." This is the logocentric predicament within which the discourses of all the human sciences are similarly trapped. We may not be able to call upon the fine art of self-conscious reading to free us from that predicament, though we *can* call upon that art to alert us fully to it. It may be—indeed *has* been—charged against Deconstructionists that for them all reality has been collapsed into the realm of writing, and that the entire realm of writing, as textuality, is read by them as one endless, infinitely regressive poem that traps us all in the rhetoric of its metaphoricity. Although Deconstruction is at great pains to emphasize its rejection of the New Criticism, the development of its fine art of reading was aided by reading methods employed by the New Criticism on individual poems. Many of the features of that long-obsolete movement have remained exemplary for American Deconstructionists as they have turned to other-than-poetic texts under the aegis of a hugely expanded notion of textuality.[8]

To the scholar committed to the priority of history, the Deconstructionist's commitment to the uninhibited resources of verbal play seems evasively ahistorical. We recall that, in assembling and complicating the interrelationships among texts, the New Historicist, in the wake of Foucault, insists on an intertextuality that shares a historical context, creating a common "discourse formation." Where there is verbal play in need of interpretation, it is referred to and limited by a narratological and metaphorical network that reflects a chronologically bound disposition of power relationships within a society; a network all of whose parts reflect the repression that is imposed by those who hold the power upon those who wish they had it and suffer for *not* having it. This sociohistorical context is all-controlling, severely limiting any verbal play within its formation.

The New Historicist is thus likely to complain that the Deconstructionist, in a sort of ahistorical mysticism about the word's powers of "dissemination," has no such contextual constraints upon the infinite regress of intertextual verbal play. It is for this reason that the New Historicist laments that, however strong and admirable its desire to do so, Deconstruction cannot with consistency make its way from texts back to the human actualities of social life as lived. Even if the Deconstructionist would want, as some of them do, to urge a sociopolitical program, the New Historicist would deny the right to such a claim because for the New Historicist Deconstruction is trapped in textuality.[9] This denial leads to the charge that Deconstruction is ultimately reducible to a late-blooming formalism; that it is, after all, just another, though more sophisticated version of escapist criticism, incapable of responding to the call for it to relate itself to sociopolitical reality.

On the other side, the Deconstructionist is likely to argue that the various forms of New Historicism, to the extent that they must find their way out of the text to claim a point of origin in the "real" power relations of a sociohistorical context, have abandoned the advantages of the poststructuralist critique, which would put in question the hidden essentialism of such a claim. For those sociopolitical structures are functioning for the New Historicist as extratextual universals, unproblematically *there,* projecting themselves outward upon the varied discursive manifestations of their culture. Because they are all-determining, these structures place a severe limit on the potentials for meaning—for verbal play—within a text. What Deconstruction can argue is that in the end there is no theoretical difference between Old and New Historicists, that one proves to be as prestructuralist as the other. For, as the argument goes, despite the vast methodological differences between them, both groups, as historicists, come to a similar resting place in the "real" historical relationships that are treated as being logically prior to discourse and as controlling the formations that discourse can take.

Here, then, is the exchange of charges—the charge by New Historicism that Deconstruction cannot avoid being detached from the social responsibility imposed by history, and the charge by Deconstruction that New Historicists must fail to pursue the poststructuralist commitment to the priority of textuality. It is to some extent reminiscent of the argument between the Old Historicism and the New Criticism and *their* exchange of charges as I described them earlier. Indeed, we should recognize this exchange as the latest version of the debate that has, throughout my survey, pitted an ahistorical concern with textual power, deeply indebted to European sources, against the native desire to tie verbal expression to its indigenous roots in a unique historical situation that, through the power generated within its moment, affects whatever it touches.

I am not suggesting that in its current version the argument of the 1940s and 1950s has not been significantly transformed, and by both sides. Nor do I mean altogether to reduce the present argument to my original set of oppositions, since we can see important theoretical advances in its present version, of course. But, despite its new face, I *am* claiming that it remains, in its root structure, essentially the same argument. For I believe the case can be made that to a great extent the same two sides are still being reflected, even in such radically altered manifestations of them.

The difficulty with a theory springing exclusively from a cultural historicism is that it *is* deterministic. On the other hand, the difficulty with a theory springing exclusively from the unrestrained readings of verbal sequences is that it gives all power to the free-wheeling creativity of both the text and the broader realm of textuality.[10] The mutually exclusive alternatives being offered by these two sets of claims seem to be either that history makes the text or that the text makes history. But clearly in some ways both claims are true, though as an absolute or exclusive claim neither is. The poem as fictional text helps create history even as, of course, history had to help create the poem. There is not any set of literary meanings *totally* imposed by history and its competing ideologies, with all of our texts doing no more than slavishly reflecting them; and, on the other side, it would be absurd to insist that the generation of textual meanings has a yield that is unrelated to what history has made available. Cultural history may supply the parameters within which a text functions, but, instead of forcing it into the categories that their historical knowledge has provided in advance, readers must always be prepared to allow the text to generate complexities that can surprise the historically conditioned expectations they bring to it.

This mutuality of dependence between these antagonists leads me to the arguments that dominate the next chapter. We find that my survey of the longstanding American debate between what, as shorthand, I am calling historicism and formalism echoes the call for literature either to reflect ideology or to resist it, with each side of the debate pressing one mission over the other. No intense reader of texts, no matter how acute, should deny the invasion of words by the assaults of power; and many Deconstructionists have demonstrated their acknowledgment of this invasion by their desire to move into the sociopolitical realm. On the other side, no one devoted to the social relevance of texts should deny the need to attend to the complications, even unpredictable ones, into which intensely interrelated words may lead. Indeed, the New Historicist is surely more aware than any earlier historicist has ever been that there may be a need—even if in the name of ideology it must be repressed—to worry about the extent to which, in the imaginative use of language, words can, or even should, be permitted and encouraged to get out of hand. As Chapter 3 indicates, Foucault himself in his earlier work gave such encouragement to literature.

So there must be—as indeed I have shown that there *has* been—a tension between these two positions as coexisting opposites: between concentrating solely on the immediate society that surrounds the text and concentrating solely on the explosive way in which language can be seen as yet once more, in this text, re-creating itself. Even the counterideologist must acknowledge that there is no use of words that does not have ideology built into it. Yet there is also reason to view the poetic fiction as using its elements to struggle against that inevitable ideological accompaniment to language, thereby, through its verbal play, seeking a freedom from monolithic tendencies of ideology.

It would be an error, one that would leave us especially exposed these days, to deny the pull of ideology, though we should also remain alert to the repressiveness that lurks within it. So there is indeed an ideological imperative that we are learning to live with; but literature, as always, has found its own subtle way to respond to it, the way of a strangely compliant resistance. It is this resistance that marks literature's special and lasting contribution to our culture, though it is the compliance that allows its contribution to appear guileless. And it is up to the critic to respond to the obligation to dwell upon that resistance as a special feature of literature. In doing so the critic also serves as a socio-historical commentator who is indispensable in leading us beyond the constraints of the discourse formation that otherwise imprisons us all. But the inflated rhetoric of this momentary conclusion rests upon the arguments that are to follow.

# 3 The Ideological Imperative and Counterideological Resistance

BESIDES THE HISTORICIST-FORMALIST OPPOSITION THAT I HAVE been considering, there is another way of viewing the opposing forces that have shaped the history of Western theory. It has been lurking in the background of my Chapters 1 and 2, and we have caught sight of it from time to time. But now it must come center stage. I refer to the continuing debate between those who interpret literary texts as instruments to serve a culture's ideology and those who treat literary texts as instruments to undermine that ideology. Once again I am making a rather crude distinction in hopes that the cleanness of its lines will help us make sense of the present state of our theoretical discourse.

It has been apparent in the preceding chapters that discussions about literary theory, or theory in general, in the West have become increasingly controlled by the role of ideology or, more precisely, by what I am terming the ideological imperative. It was not always thus; indeed, in its current form it is a relatively recent development, and one that we may well want to question, as theory in the past has questioned earlier versions of it.

As I approach the debate, what seems to be at issue are the roles attributed to literature and to ideology in sociopolitical repression, and on the other side, the roles attributed to literature and to ideology in liberating us from repression. These are the several grounds of the quarrels that in the United States are continuing at a very rapid rate, indeed rabid as well as rapid. Their consequences will dictate the shape of humanities for years to come, if indeed there is still to be a humanities in any form that we could recognize as such.

Surely the dominant tendency of literary criticism and literary theory in the West since the earliest hints of them in Plato has been to see the literary work as one of many direct reflections of the cultural values that surround it and through its author give it its life. That dominance has persisted, though with some notable and influential exceptions, throughout the centuries. At the outset of the Western theoretical tradition, Plato had continually insisted on literature's, or—more broadly—art's mimetic character: the extent to which it was an imitation of the world outside, although for Plato, of course, it was for ill rather than for good that it imitated the outside world. Plato was out to attack literature and saw its imitative function as morally and politically dangerous. In attacking it he created a semiotic whose dualistic character would shape the work of critics for centuries, indeed for millennia. Those who followed Plato, whether as his disciples attacking literature or as his antagonists defending it, took from him a belief in the one-to-one reducibility between the literary text and the larger social text to which it relates as a sign to a referent, as microcosm to macrocosm, as the text to its context. As I have said, this is clearly the dominant tendency throughout literary history.

At the same time, in Plato's antagonism toward literature, indeed in his moral rejection of it, he also revealed the very opposite tendency. We find, in his distaste for literature, a companion concern about the capacity of literature—or rather, its power—to subvert rather than to reflect the moral truths of its culture. We recall that, in Plato's attack upon the lowly worldly objects that literature as an art could and did imitate, he worried about the extent to which literature, like the arts generally, was necessarily diverted from what should have been its objective—the potential imitation of the true and the morally good and, from Plato's point of view, the politically necessary. He saw the arts, instead, as subverting through distortion what should have been their proper object and mission.

This charge attributed to literature a subversive relation to the culture it should have reflected: an unpredictable, potentially dangerous, and hence politically unreliable or even irresponsible function with respect to the ideologies that culture would represent as its truth—indeed that, for Plato, culture should be *compelled* to represent. It is to this subversive function that, for example, Saint Augustine, as Plato's late heir, referred when, looking upon his own sinful history, he confessed a moral-religious failure deriving from his yielding to an aesthetic response: "I who wept for Dido slain." For this Platonist the emotional cost to the reader of the death of Dido in Virgil is a price that a proper morality cannot afford. It is a subversion of the proper relationship between blind human sympathy and divinely guided moral judgment.

This awareness of literature's potential to have subversive consequences is a minor refrain that accompanies, as it throws doubt upon, the mimetic tradition across the centuries. But this potential function did come most strenuously into its own in the last two centuries, this time with approval rather than rejection. From romanticism through the movement we call high modernism, which finishes roughly in the middle of our own century, literature is celebrated for its subversive mission as the voice of the private, subjective dissident in the author. This voice finds itself embodied in specially formed texts, which undermine the straightforward arguments of a culture's governing discourse. The case comes to be made for literary texts as language systems of their own, whatever the cost may be to the confidently held universal propositions that are enunciated in the verbal structures that surround them. This is a special role that had been enunciated for literature from romanticism through high modernism, but the story of postmodernism in the last several decades is the story of how extensively, deeply, and angrily this case for literature has come to be widely rejected by Continental and American criticism alike.

These, then, are the two major tendencies that I am examining, even though I can do so only at the cost of crudely oversimplifying our critical history. The first sees in literature the reinforcement and reflection of ideological discourse, and the second sees in literature the resistance to it, if not the utter subversion of it. My objective here is to isolate a certain continuity in the second, the counterideological tradition, in literary theory, a tradition that is in danger of being snuffed out by the ideological emphasis of recent years. But I must get to the second by way of the first, by tracing, throughout the history of our criticism, the several obvious and standard ways in which literary works have been treated as no more than essentially undistorted reflections of their surrounding social and cultural contexts.

For summary purposes I can distinguish within the history of the first and dominant tendency two quite different subdivisions, which, despite their differences, similarly require a reflective function for literature: the realistic claim for imitation and the morally didactic claim; or, as it has frequently been put, the call for literature to imitate what is and the call for literature to imitate what the poet or the critic decides ought to be. In the one, the literary work is asked to imitate, and thus to subscribe to, the world that exists outside it and to refer directly to that world (the assumption being that such a neutral world is unproblematically there and can be referred to); and in the other, the literary work is asked to refer, and thus to subscribe to, some set of moral necessities, those moral propositions that a culture's ideology holds out as its highest ideals.

The first of these, the realistic claim, is obvious enough and has been urged at many times in the history of our criticism. It is the bulwark of most of the theories advanced in support of historical criticism, although, because it does not question the neutral, objective reality of history, it represents what in the preceding chapter I called the "Old," in contrast to the "New," Historicism. But I set that distinction aside for now. The most extreme and thus most easily cited example of this simple claim of literary realism—of the literary text as an undistorted reflection of a surrounding historical instant of its culture—is that which is attributed to the French nineteenth-century historian of literature Hippolyte Taine, in his positivistic and hence deterministic insistence on reducing everything that goes on in the literary work to the surrounding "race, moment, and milieu" of the historical context that gives rise to it.

In this extreme form, if we are given a full report of what a culture is like at any given moment, we should just about be able to predict what its literature will say, since the meanings and values represented in the literary work are to be seen as having a one-to-one relationship to the meanings and values of the society or social group out of which it emerges. If the signs within a literary work are a collection of an *a,* a *b,* a *c,* a *d,* and so forth, then each *a* is seen as responsible to the matching *a′* that is external to the work—each *b* to the *b′,* each *c* to the *c′,* each *d* to the *d′,* and so forth—rather than responsible to the internal relations that language creates within and among those several signs.

What is being argued is that the literary work is a window and that the signs inside relate transparently to their sources in the realities outside. It is an obvious enough claim and has been made from Plato onward all the way down to American literary realism, even in its extreme attempt to press realism in fiction to the "slice of life" novel, as we used to call it. There are many versions of this claim to literary realism through two millennia, all of them resting on a simple representational view of the literary text's semiotic role—its role as a collection of referential signs—as it relates to its societal context. It is a claim, or even often an almost axiomatic assumption, that never seems to die altogether. It survives even into modern popular book-reviewing in the recurrent desire for the individual literary text somehow to be "true to life."[1]

This is the first of the two subdivisions within what I have set apart as the mimetic tendency, the assumption of a one-to-one reflective relationship between the literary work and a claimed outside reality, whether in the world or in the world of words. The second subdivision is the morally didactic, in which the literary work is given the primary objective of persuading and teaching, since it is seen as directly reflective of one or another moral ideology through which a culture, whether dominant or repressed, projects the values that any of its individuals, as members of one or another of its social groups, *ought* to hold and *ought* to promulgate. Because the moral universal is often accorded a metaphysical sanction—indeed, an ontological grounding—in the nature of things, this sort of criticism may also be seen as mimetic in its didactics, though what is being imitated transcends the visible reality of our experience, pointing rather to its ontological grounding in an invisible realm.[2]

We find versions of this tendency in all the Neo-Platonists from the Renaissance through neoclassicism and from Victorian moralism to both American "Neo-Humanists" and early American Marxists.[3] In all of these there is an assumption of an authoritarian rule over discourse by a propositional reality that exists outside and prior to discourse. And modernist criticism of the mid-century seemed successfully to have discredited what appeared to be the simplism of these formulations as they imposed themselves on the ambitions of the literary text to generate its meanings.

In recent years, however, a more sophisticated variety of this kind of reading, which ties the text to ideology, has been called for. This reading probes for an ideological *sub*text lurking beneath the fictional surface of every text, revealing the motives that propel its discourse, serving one or another set of ideological presuppositions. The apparent text, which offers itself to our superficial perception as all there is, should rather be seen as a potential *de*ception in its rhetorical act of selling us on the hidden text that, without the social critic's help, we may not be able to dig out from beneath the text. Thus every so-called literary text, or indeed any kind of text, is to be unmasked as yet another linguistic agent of power and hence revealed as a surreptitious reflection of one or another ideological structure.[4]

To reread a text in a way that substitutes the subtext and its hidden motivation for the apparent text and *its* apparent (and deceptive) intention — however subtle those rereadings may be — is still to rest on the reductive insistence that the literary work is a programmatic reflection, a fictional, allegorical mirroring, of a firmly held agenda. What we have is a theory of interpretation that has properly been termed a hermeneutic of suspicion: however innocent, however apolitical, the text may appear to be, every text is indeed in the service of an ideology that hides itself from us, except that the political critic, working with an assumption of the primacy of the political unconscious, can reveal it. The text, then, must be seen as emerging out of the reality of a society and its power relations; as being authorized and thus as being shaped by these power relations, as the rhetorical end of this deterministic chain.

So much for this much too compact and simplified examination of this still post-Platonic way of reading, the widely varied ways in which criticism — as long as it is ascetic in the limitations it places on what literature can do to us and for us — has treated literature as a reflection of, a coming after, the "realities" of the worlds or the words that exist before and outside its own verbal structure. One way or another this is the kind of thinking *against* which the counterideological tradition that is my subject defines

itself—although this contrary tradition can also be traced back
to Plato, who gave it life, even while condemning the subversive
character of literature because it led us away from conceiving the
world as his moral universals would have it. Out of Plato's insistence that the literary work could not imitate those universals
arose his conviction that its lowly mimetic character, its devotion
to imperfect particulars, could not help but subvert them. It is
not at all difficult to turn the political reading back on Plato to
find *his* subtext, one that serves the reactionary tendencies of the
Athenian state by providing it with a metaphysic that authorizes
a rigid hierarchy of sociopolitical classes. And his static rational-
ism could lead him to the fear of literature as subversion—the
fear of a literature that instead of reflecting his ideology puts ideology into question.

All through the centuries, for most of the history of literature
and criticism in the West, there has been this minority tradition
of a reading that would treat literature not as a reflection and reinforcement, but as an undermining, of the ideas that sustain the
societal context. In our century, through the delicate analysis of
verbal subtleties, this way of reading seeks, then claims to find,
and proceeds to exploit ironies that run counter to what would
seem to be a single-minded argument representing exclusively
one or another of the surrounding cultural discourses. It draws
its counterideological power from the assumption that ideology
tends to speak in not more than one voice. In a culture there are
many voices, each of them representing an ideology that seeks to
guide action in one given direction rather than another in its
quest for power, and thus each of them emphasizing a single line
of argument. We have seen, in examining the first tradition, that
the call for literature to reflect ideology is a call for literature, like
any other discourse that speaks its culture's voice, also to reflect
only a single line of argument.

This second tradition, which looks for a literature that undermines an ideology instead of reinforcing it, is seeking, by reading
very closely, to emphasize the way in which a text that seems to
move in one direction, reflecting and supporting a given ideological structure, has within it those elements that subvert what
appears to be the dominant tendency of the work and turn it
against itself. This reading claims to discover the full range of

meanings that sustains a literary text and resists being reduced to one rhetorical line that moves exclusively in one direction or another. Instead of those windows I spoke of, where the *a,* the *b,* the *c,* and the *d* of the literary work each points directly and transparently to the realities that are its archetypes outside the work, the theorists emerging from this tradition would have us see the literary work as an enclosed set of internalizing mirrors bouncing meanings and images between and among themselves. These internalized interactions are seen as shutting off the work by creating a structure of complexities that eludes any attempt to make it into an ideology's servant.

Not that ideological critics cannot turn any work into the servant of their ideology, but counterideological critics would find such readings insufficient and indelicate—not responsive enough to the complex dimensions and contrary directions that they see interacting dynamically within the literary work. It is as if one blackens the outside of the glass of a window, shutting off the outside world, converting window to mirror, displaying a set of internal reflections maddeningly, and inconsequentially, multiplying one another.[5] Any reading that leads to this multiplication of complexity, of internalizing reflections within reflections, would resist the authoritarian rule of propositions that, according to this tradition at least, tries to repress opposition. Each side of such mutually exclusive oppositions is authoritarian in that it seeks to govern discourse absolutely, repressing anything that does not reinforce the single direction being pursued.

This view, that the literary text presents a self-complicating subversion of an ideological structure of argumentative discourse, can be traced back to the ancient war between the poets and the philosophers that Plato so forcefully addressed. Indeed, Plato's attack on literature was his attack on the poets from the philosophers' side, as an answer to the irrational threat he saw them posing to a fixed social order and the rational structure of propositions that supported it. He was deeply concerned about the extent to which his Greek audience might take its philosophy from Homer, whose writings Plato considered morally dangerous in their devotion to the complex characters and stories of myth. The *Iliad* and the *Odyssey* were just too complicated, had too many countermovements undermining the call to perfection and too much catering to human emotions, for them to be trusted as moral guides for the reader. It would be politically safer for Homer to be exiled and the philosopher-king allowed to rule in the name of unchallenged ideology (though Plato would prefer to call it "reason"). Plato may have attributed "real" reference to poetic signs, as mimetic, but he saw them using their worldly objects to divert us from the ideal realm, thereby becoming didactically harmful.[6] Thus Plato had to warn us against the poets, who as free spirits let loose the untamed and imperfect fables that could undermine the static, authoritarian social order he would establish. And I guess they did — and have continued to do so.

I move now to later versions of the counterideological tendency. In the past two centuries the development of the tradition of interpretation that is associated with the "sublime" has increasingly disrupted the role of orderly "beauty" and encouraged less rationally controlled readings. Beginning in late antiquity with Longinus, the "sublime" finally attained an important place in eighteenth-century thinking about art as a challenge to the dominance of mimetic theory, that is, the theory of literature as a reflection of the extraliterary. This was the period when mimetic theory, now in its neoclassical version, was in many quarters more tightly constraining than perhaps it had ever been. As a counter to the notion of art as all reason and order in subordination to rational and orderly thought, the doctrine of the "sublime," which had become fairly common currency since Boileau's translation of Longinus into French almost a century earlier, was systematically reintroduced by Edmund Burke to undo the cool, easy dominion of the "beautiful." The sublime was seen as that which jars us, which terrifies us, which destroys the security of that universal order of things about which the eighteenth century seemed so confident. Of course, Burke derived his use of the term from Longinus, another ancient whose work increased its influence in the late eighteenth century, when romanticism was ready to flower and the rational order of the beautiful was ready to be undermined.

From Longinus through to Burke, then from Burke to Kant and to the romantics, and from them to the high modernists and even beyond to thinkers as postmodern as Jean-François Lyotard, there develops this loose, antisystematic, emotionally driven alternative to the more straightforward, rational versions of how texts should relate to the rule of philosophic systems and their straightforward propositions. It claims for the sublime a way of freeing language from such stringencies in order to explode what is seen as too thin a sense of order, such as the beautiful (as conceived in the eighteenth century) would reflect.

What lies behind this alternative is the assumption that experience is messy and that the order of our discourse and the order of our ideologies are simply too simple for the complexities of human experience that they must accommodate. Thus, this thinking goes, we may need these practical simplicities, as well as the conceptual discourse that both governs and follows from them, to function in our everyday living; but if, more contemplatively, we want to confront fully how life is with us, then we need to go beyond them. Literature and, indeed, the arts generally, are viewed as the only avenues leading us to explore these complexities. To this end the arts should work to violate, subvert, if not altogether explode, our ideological claims, or at least our confidence in them.

From the perspective of this interpretive tradition, we would still look at the dominant discourse of a culture as repressive, as exclusionary and authoritarian, but we now would see literature as the liberating voice—liberation in the name of the individual, of the dissident. This tradition persists at least through the middle of our own century, and in another form even afterward. In the form it takes as the ultimate fruition of romantic theory, it attributes to the proper poem a unique complex of possible meanings that subverts any would-be exclusionary meaning that we might, in our political haste, seek to extrapolate from the poem—a meaning (this theory argues) such as would be found and *can* be found in nonliterature.

The argument for the independence of the literary from the conceptual—and, indeed, its priority to the conceptual—was strengthened by the earliest definitions of the "aesthetic" in the attempt, since the mid-eighteenth century, to establish the aesthetic as a discipline. In the two centuries of thought that followed—into the mid-twentieth century—an increasingly special role has been claimed for the aesthetic, which has been associated with "imagination" or "intuition" in distinction from "understanding" or "reason." This role was defined as a privileged alternative to the role of conceptual thinking. From Baumgarten to Mendelssohn to Kant to Coleridge and finally to the New Critics, the aesthetic, intimately related to our senses as immediate receptors, was accorded a primary—which is to say a preconceptual—place in the epistemological sequence governing human cognition.

The claim of the independence of the aesthetic from concepts is central to developments leading to high modernism. For example, it becomes the very center of the theorizing of Benedetto Croce. Descended from nineteenth-century German organicism, Croce becomes the leading proponent of the aesthetic as a mode of experience at the close of the last century and the beginning of this one. Much later, Eliseo Vivas, often referred to as the aesthetician of the New Criticism in the 1940s and 1950s, privileges the aesthetic—hence, in the verbal arts, the literary—because he sees it as dealing with and revealing "the primary data of human experience." That word "data" is used by him in its technical epistemological sense as that which is "given" to the senses before being acted upon by our reasoning and generalizing—that is, by our conceptual—faculties.

This claim of priority, which leads to a special epistemological licensing of the aesthetic, is a major point of attack by recent critics of modernism and its preoccupation with the aesthetic. For such critics, who once more take up the notion of the arts as a coming-after, a reflection, of the sociocultural context, the conceptual is the home of the ideological, and for them nothing is prior to the force of ideology in exerting control over all our visions and our judgments, including, of course, the aesthetic. Working from the premise of Fredric Jameson's notion of the political unconscious as the primary, if secret, agent behind all our discourse, this recent mode of critical thinking sees the aesthetic as no more than a deceptive lure in political manipulation, a lure that masks itself in the claim to an innocent epistemological primacy despite its concealed role as the servant of all-dominating concepts.

The disguise of function serves in an opposite way for those defending the priority of the aesthetic. As one of the arts instead of just one among many uses of language, the literary was to defend itself from being employed as a secret instrument substituting for — and in this way serving — conceptual, and hence ideological, argument. From the romantics to the New Criticism, only the works of poets, in a sort of prepolitical purity, were granted untainted visionary powers, to which they were to remain faithful. Indeed, the literary criticism of these theorists, and others like them, usually consisted of their attempts to show how the verbal, tropological, and narratological relations they were examining in their privileged texts resisted any absorption into concepts. This was the ground of the dichotomy, long pursued in the organicist tradition and culminating in high modernism, between symbol and allegory — between, that is, the monistic density of the self-contained sign and the dualistic referral of the sign outward to the external concept it reflected. And the honorific title of the proper poem was to be bestowed only upon the symbolic, with the allegory consigned to what Croce termed "the intellectualist error," which comes, as he says, from the aesthetic functioning as a disguised form of the conceptual.

What I am tracing as the counterideological tradition in aesthetics develops in literary criticism by means of German doctrines of romantic irony, as well as Coleridge's derivative claim that the poetic imagination was found in "the balance or reconciliation of opposite or discordant qualities."[7] The poem was encouraged to create its own irreducible complex of autonomous meanings by entering the realm of self-contradiction in order to free itself from the limited, unilinear way in which nonpoetic discourse seems to intend to mean. This complicating inclusiveness of the web of poetic discourse gives it license to stand as a subverting as well as a self-subverting critique of that exclusionary discourse with which we are condemned to live daily — a discourse that, without poetry, is used by forces in culture to allow them to work their way with us, just as they make us work for them.

In our own century, I can trace many versions, growing out of several theoretical varieties, that, despite their otherwise important differences, unite in making the case for a counterideological aesthetic. For example, there are the claims made as early as 1915 by a relatively obscure thinker (obscure now, though not in his own day), Bernard Bosanquet, in his book *Three Lectures on Aesthetic*. There he argues for what he calls "difficult beauty" as art's highest achievement, with its difficulty seen in what he calls its "intricacy," its "tension." He makes these claims three or four decades before the heyday of the New Criticism. It is evident that for Bosanquet "difficulty" in art is a measure of a density of meaning in art that is unavailable to nonart.

In their attempt to extend such a concept to practical criticism, the New Critics literalized this notion by emphasizing the verbal complexities of ambiguity, paradox, and irony, all of these suggesting to them a counterideological complicating of normal meanings—and the straightforward arguments behind them—in the literary work. These ideas come to the New Criticism in the United States through two later nineteenth- and earlier twentieth-century traditions, one of them Continental, one of them English.

On the Continent a major source is Arthur Schopenhauer, who borrowed from Far Eastern thought in order to enlarge upon and transform Immanuel Kant's notion of disinterestedness. Finding art to be an indispensable aid in achieving what is for him the ideal human objective, the transcendence of all our private desires, Schopenhauer defined art by its power to provide an escape from the ruthless hegemony of the "will" (the will—as Kant's "practical reason"—serving our subjective interests and thus destroying the possibility of our being disinterested). In the wake of Schopenhauer, theorists attributed to literature, in contrast to other discourses as discourses of the will, a collision of meanings that precludes action because it precludes the unquestioning, authoritarian, unilinear direction needed to stimulate action, which is seen as invariably will-driven.

From Schopenhauer by way of the early Nietzsche to Henri Bergson, the arts alone are given the power to pierce the "veil of Maya," a notion clearly derived from Eastern philosophy.[8] In order to make action possible, it is claimed that we interpose the veil of Maya between ourselves as perceivers and the complexity of our experience, which defies those simplistic reductions produced by our normal language in the service of the clean decisiveness required for action. It is the need to act that produces this veil, which we cannot break through because we allow the simple rationale for action to go without challenge. Hence our need for the veil, but also our need for the role of the arts to pierce it. Bergson tells us that the poet, as artist, must break through the veil constituted by the stereotypes of our normal discourse, which is needed to produce and account for our usual activities. Coleridge had a phrase for it a century earlier: "the film of familiarity and selfish solicitude," with the "film" his equivalent of the "veil."[9] Here is the point of union, the notion that joins the Continental to the English tradition. And Coleridge, with his almost complete indebtedness to German writers, is the appropriate figure to represent that union.

From Bergson to the Russian Formalists, what lies behind this pattern of thinking about literature and what continues to control its theoretical development is an unquestioned assumption that there is a clear distinction between "normal" and "poetic" discourse (the latter including all self-conscious fictions, whether in verse or prose). The poetic arises out of the violation of the way in which discourse normally works. The poet must distort verbal sequence, complicate verbal meanings, give constitutive power to tropes in order to force language to represent what for normal language would seem to be unrepresentable. It then has the chance to become a form of discourse that can reveal what in our experience is otherwise hidden behind the veil of Maya.

Clearly, the opposition is the familiar one, developed for the arts most forcefully by Bergson, between action and contemplation, in which the first is identified with normal discourse and the second with the discourses of art. It is by means of that opposition that this tradition realizes itself. As its argument goes, as long as language is to serve action, as long as language is to restrict itself in order to serve the ideology of one or another group, it cannot be fashioned into an instrument beyond these limited capacities, and we cannot use it to pierce the veil. Presumably the vision into what is beyond the veil, which the capacities of poetic language can open for us, will likely prove to be paralyzing in that the unfolding complications it reveals would block any clean line of action. But if we want the freedom of pure contemplation, even at the expense of the ability to act, then we must have the freedom not only to look at every movement in language but also to entertain every countermovement that every movement surreptitiously contains within itself. For these critics it is poems alone, among the verbal arts, that permit this freedom.

Thus, by separating the modes of discourse, the literary from the normal, and by attributing this privileged role to the literary alone as the discourse that undermines — by exceeding — the way in which discourse seems normally intended to function, Bergson helped create the kind of criticism that we later, in our own century, came in the United States to call the New Criticism, which exaggerated this attempt to grant to literature the license whereby it could nourish its negative relationship to ideological certainty. For it is *un*certainty that is cultivated once we want to be free to contemplate the human condition without being forced by ideological constraints to march off in one direction or another. So much for the Continental sources of this chain of argument.

From the English side there is another influence, the one I have already observed in Coleridge, which sponsored in Matthew Arnold later in the nineteenth century an attempt to preserve a unique cultural role for poetry, a role outside the path of more undeviating roads to our daily truths.[10] Separating knowledge of fact from emotion and separating also the human faculties addressed to each of these, Arnold called upon poetry to minister to our emotions, saving it as *the* discourse that could humanize meaning as a verbal system, turning inward as it rejects the external pressures of the cold, knowledge-ridden obligations of reference. Poetry makes an appeal that violates the cold world of universal propositional truths that have no emotional meaning for the individual, and through that violation makes it possible for us to grasp a world that has in it those more things in heaven and earth than are dreamt of in any of our (rational) philosophies.

As a follower of Matthew Arnold, I. A. Richards made available to the New Critics a mediation, though also a distortion, of Arnold. Richards defined poetry through its capacity, as an "emotive" rather than a "referential" mode of discourse, to undo the clean lines that controlled the point-by-point reference from the sign to the real thing according to the semiotic principle that governed the operation of referential discourse.[11] For Richards the instrument for this undoing, this transformation of discursive functioning, was irony, which grew out of his work into becoming a major feature of the New Criticism and beyond. Richards defined irony as "the bringing in of the opposite, the complementary impulses."[12] It is the role of the poet somehow to find within the unilinear rhetorical tendency of any discourse this opposite and yet complementary impulse. It is this propensity for doubling that distinguishes the poem's discourse from the way normal discourse—that is, discourse in the service of action through being discourse in the service of reference—can operate.

The model New Critic was Cleanth Brooks,[13] who, following the lead of Richards, played up the poem's system of internal relations as a sealed context of mutually reflecting mirrors (to use my own earlier metaphor) that precludes any attempt at unqualified reference.[14] The reflexive character of the poem's irony produces in it a self-irony as well: it bounces back on itself, again and again—chasing its meanings into an abyss, we might say today. Through such devices poetry works its complications upon the normal reach and depth of how we read, and thus how we talk and how we see.

Richards had insisted that the poem, by means of its irony, functions to block action through producing an equilibrium that counters every impulse to act in one direction with an impulse to act in the opposite direction. In Brooks irony leads to the claim that every would-be meaning in the poem is confronted by its self-contradiction, a would-be meaning in the opposite direction. This irony expands the poem into an unstable context that defies reason by seeking to hold at once both the meaning *and* its contradiction within a single verbal sequence that inside the poem makes sense even though we cannot, outside the poem, quite say what that sense is. The counterideological thrust of this entire tradition is perhaps most fully witnessed in Brooks's explications of individual literary texts.

This concentration upon the poem as a unique, privileged mode of discourse, a construct that, through self-enclosure, can create its own special meaning, pretty well dies with the New Critics. Those textualists we have come to call Deconstructionists are probably even more careful readers, constantly reading movements as undone by countermovements within a single sequence of words. But unlike the New Critics, who reserved such treatment for poetic texts alone, the Deconstructionists, working from a theory about how textuality itself, in all its manifestations, functions, range well beyond the narrowly literary and work their reading methods on all sorts of texts, since with them all discourse has become equally, and similarly, eligible for this kind of analysis.

No one more influentially opposed the restriction of New Critical "irony" to poems than the leading Deconstructionist in the United States, Paul de Man. It was the purpose of de Man's readings to seek out the self-deconstructive disposition of the text—just about any text. It was his way of "reading against the grain." He reads a text, but within it his rhetorical reading finds an undertext that is also a countertext, one that allows him to read against the grain even as he reads with it. He would accept the challenge of almost any text—no matter how apparently single-minded, how unilinear, it appeared to be—to find the countergrain lying within. So fierce is de Man's antagonism to the claim of unified meaning, so strong his own commitment to trace a regressive dispersion of mutually antagonistic meanings, that his primary argument against the formalist (which for him was the New Critical) criticism of poems is its quest for an ultimate unity, for a reconciliation of disparate materials.[15]

One of de Man's major essays has him taking on, at the nonpoetic extreme, the work of John Locke, whose argument usually has been treated, and deservedly so, as one of the most straightforwardly and unambiguously rational in the history of British philosophy.[16] But de Man's explorations find Locke's text dependent upon a series of tropes that complicate its rhetoric by undercutting the very argument that Locke appears to be so single-mindedly making, thus denying stability even to *that* sort of text.

There is no question that the force of Deconstruction was strenuously anti–New Critical in that it consistently opposed the New Critical setting aside and privileging of the literary. Nevertheless, de Man's principal method of reading, even as he applies it to nonliterary as well as to literary texts, seems to have much in common with the counterideological character of the New Critical method of reading poems, an interpretive method that we have here seen developing from romanticism to the middle of this century.[17] In Deconstruction the range of objects has been greatly enlarged—the kinds of texts that are admitted are almost without limit—but the reading method is not quite unfamiliar. Now the entire realm of textuality has become subject to what we used to think of as exclusively literary analysis. So all texts come to be treated as counterideological; indeed, textuality, as it is conceived in accordance with de Man's claims for the rhetoric of reading, is in itself (in its *essence,* dare we see him as implying?) a counterideological process.[18]

In the work of de Man and his followers a question arises—what may appear to be an uncertainty or at least an ambiguity—as we observe their interpretations of texts: Does the text at hand, in its apparently unilinear intention, require a deconstructive reading to open it up, or is the text itself shrewdly *self-*deconstructive, requiring acute readers only to follow along, pointing out what the text has, in its half-concealed way, already performed? The followers of de Man could claim easily to dissolve that uncertainty by denying that it is an ambiguity: They could argue that it is not the text but the unilinear and logocentric way in which Locke's text, or others similarly "transparent," is usually read that needs to be deconstructed—to be read against the grain—in order to show the rest of us, because we tend to read it otherwise, how that text *can* be seen as deconstructing itself. *Any* text.

Without disagreeing, I would still want to argue for some soft distinctions. I would claim that the literary work is distinguished by openly seeking that self-deconstruction, leading even a pre-Deconstructionist reading of it, merely as a commentary on what is going on in it, to become a Deconstructionist reading as it simply traces the complexities that the poetic fiction has the leisure, the ideological freedom, to present. The poetic fiction thus can create a network of cross-meanings and cross-purposes that leads even the straightforward commentator to deconstruct every potential ideological construct in the mere process of accounting for what the literary text is manifestly doing. By contrast, the ostensibly nonfictional text, seen as created in response to an author's logically ordered and unilinear rhetorical intention, must have that intentional structure deconstructed in the act of interpretation if we are to find counterintentions within it and thus break it away from its author and from the entire realm of intentionality.

For ostensibly nonfictional texts, then, there is a critical distance between the text as it can be read deconstructively and the text as it is seen, conventionally, within its discipline—seen predeconstructively—as asking to be read. I argue that this distance is reduced almost to the vanishing point by the poetic fiction, which seems to wear on its face, to quote Wolfgang Iser, "the simultaneity of the mutually exclusive."[19] Such intratextual features of the poetic fiction make it an emblem of textuality at large, make it a micro-text, which can serve as a model of how other texts, presumably nonfictional, can be seen as performing. Following the lead of poetic fictions, we can deconstruct other sorts of texts by searching in them for those countertendencies that, contrary to the institutional blindness that dictates our usual ways of reading them, may induce us to see them as deconstructing themselves. In leading us toward those readings of such texts, Deconstructionists are adapting a reading method prompted by how literary texts ask to be read. So these serve as exemplary texts, master texts that display those tendencies for which, in other texts, the reader's own deconstructive subtlety is required in order that this self-deconstructive potential may be found to be a characteristic of discourse itself.

It is on these grounds that I argue that, even now in these poststructuralist days, there is continuing reason to resist obliterating the distinction between the ostensibly unilinear in discourse and the poetically fictional—in my terms here, between the ideological and the counterideological. Indeed, it is, both theoretically and practically, useful as well as reasonable to do so. I want to be clear about the fact that I am not trying in some archaic way to argue for a generic difference between poems and nonpoems, but rather to allow for elements of poetic fictions that the keen interpreter is alerted to find (or to claim to find) in whatever texts those elements may modify, or perhaps even take over. I am thoroughly aware that, once having said this much, I may be giving away the chance for making any workable distinction between discursive kinds since any shrewdly deconstructive reader can come up with these elements everywhere in texts. To acknowledge as much is to acknowledge only that any distinction would be a matter of delicate degrees rather than of kind, and that, except for the obvious extremes at either end of the spectrum leading from poetic fictions to their discursive opposites, we require readerly good sense and many arguments about who has it in particular cases in order to make our judgments and make them stick. But that is no more than we have ever required of competing interpretations seeking our assent.

De Man's treatment of the passage from Locke exemplifies his refusal to allow even an apparently single-minded text to evade ambiguity, as if a potential ambiguity lurks in the very essence of language functioning. There is just no provision in de Man for a discourse that can unambiguously express an ideology; any that seems to do so could be shown by him to undercut that expression in the very act of making it. It is this position in de Man-style reading that has, by way of opposition, led to the strongly anti-Deconstructionist flavor of recent American theory, in which the political interest has been rising markedly. The more ideological this politicized theory has become, the more it has complained that Deconstruction—especially of the sort exemplified by de Man—exceeded even the New Criticism in its counterideological bent, precisely because it extended its coverage to texts of every sort, including even would-be political texts.

Accordingly, recent politically motivated theorists see Deconstruction as exposing its own unacknowledged formalism, which extended the New Criticism's, indeed which functions as the furthest extension of the counterideological tendency I have been tracing. If discourse does not permit authors to make an undeviating ideological point and to use their texts to call us to an undeviating course of action, *without* somehow having their language itself work against what they ostensibly intend to do, then there is no way for discourse not to be self-deconstructive. And, as the result of a language engaged in play within its own capacities of meaning, there is no structure of meaning that cannot be undermined by itself, or at least that cannot be read as undermining itself, as putting itself in question (in a favorite phrase of Deconstructionists). Language has been forced to say more, or other, than it apparently intended to, thanks to a much more complicated reading process than anyone who wants language to serve ideology could possibly permit.

As the narrative of Chapter 2 tried to show, whereas Deconstructionists thought of themselves as having succeeded the New Critics by thoroughly rejecting them, the more recent sociopolitical theorists have seen Deconstructionists as those who imperialized New Critical methods by taking a procedure that had been modestly confined to poetry and imposing it on all the varieties of discourse, an extension that can only increase the frustration of anyone for whom discourse is to function primarily, and ultimately, in order to serve ideological purposes. These newer sociopolitical theorists have returned to what I at the start of this chapter traced as the first of the major theoretical traditions of interpretation. I refer, of course, to the long dominant—and, until the late sixties, for some time discredited—way of treating literary texts: as immediate reflections of the "realities" imposed by the powers that control their social environment and hence their language.

These theorists are again putting texts into the service of ideology and hence of action, forcing them to override any potentially troublesome, and perhaps paralyzing, complexities within them. Indeed, they condemn the "mandarin" pursuit of complexity as an excuse for evading the directness of action and, consequently, as a surreptitious way of serving the power structure.[20] In declining, by obfuscating, the clean choice between alternative actions, it is argued, the pursuit of complexity removes discourse from the disjunctive necessities of decision-making. Since these theorists call for a reading that is to be controlled by a "hermeneutic of suspicion," one may imagine how politically suspicious they must be of this version of Deconstruction.

Before concluding this survey, I must briefly mention some moves that would join the two alternatives I have been showing as opposed throughout the history of Western theory. These moves would see literature as serving social objectives, but only by way of the counterideological emphasis that I have associated with the aesthetic. I am thinking of recently influential theorists such as Mikhail Bakhtin and Jean-François Lyotard. (Of course, Bakhtin's work is many decades old, though some years back it was suddenly revitalized and made available to postmodern theory, after having been largely ignored.) Their attempt to make this counterideological, and hence subversive, characteristic of at least some texts[21] serve a social and political purpose may these days be the most promising version of the counterideological tradition that I have been tracing. In their privileging of the counterideological, both Bakhtin and Lyotard in their different ways may be seen as reinforcing the tradition of the aesthetic—perhaps despite their intentions, which lead them to be highly distrustful of the aesthetic.

As a way of emphasizing the dialogical character of literature, Bakhtin frees it—especially in the novel with its multiplication of incompatible genres—to revel in the carnivalesque. This is a textual force that, like the ritual of carnival in an authoritarian society—that momentary suspension of hierarchy and repressive distinctions—throws up in the air a variety of otherwise incompatible possibilities, for the occasion free of authoritarian regulation and its ideologically controlled structure.

One may grant that the dominant culture may well be using the potential subversion arising out of its indulgence of carnival to demonstrate its awesome power, which can domesticate even the most unruly of its subjects and render them harmless by authorizing and even ritualizing them, bringing them into the consent calendar that patterns the lives of the governed. Nevertheless, through that momentary indulgence, the Bakhtinian carnivalesque opens a culture's vision to what ideology, as a repressive agent, would condemn as the forbidden: seeking to reinforce itself by allowing what is not permitted representation to be represented, the power structure allows us to see with other eyes than its own. And however encapsulated the moment of carnival, however harmless it has been rendered, what has been seen may be remembered and may someday have its unmanageable consequences. Just so can literature, as long as it works dialogically, manipulate a culture's ruling discourse in a surreptitious disruption of the usual ways that discourse operates and maintains its authorized meanings, which is to say, its dominant ideology. And just so can it be the instrument of our seeing anew, freeing our vision and encouraging us to disrupt the trim discursive lines of authority.

In a similar vein, Lyotard seeks to invalidate all "master nar-
ratives" in order to allow autonomy to the little stories, *"les pe-
tites histoires,"* that resist adaptation into a universal story, indeed, that cannot be made to serve any generalized structure of
meaning and, beyond that, any unified plan of action. Through
such little stories and their resistance to the rationality of a master narrative, Lyotard resurrects the notion of the sublime as a
violation of philosophic order. The sublime, now become a postmodern virtue, shines through the jagged edges of piecemeal
"phrases," which are to satisfy us in a world that must learn to
do without the finality of whole "sentences." As moments of the
postmodern sublime, these mini-subversions go on and on, and
the carnival of little stories, each with its small but unyielding
resistance, overwhelms any master narrative that would claim
control over all little stories.

The counterideological thrust of what I have been treating as
the tradition of the aesthetic thus receives, however obliquely,
this postmodernist blessing, the call to a continuing resistance.
In emphasizing these scattered autonomies, Lyotard, like Bakhtin before him, is, through his own master metaphor, of course
speaking politically. The celebration of the small power of an
uncontrollable number of individual secessions proclaims a kind
of literary anarchy, not altogether unrelated to Leon Trotsky's
notion of "permanent revolution." Or might we, through Bakhtin, call it permanent carnival?

Through the varied participants we have observed in the tradition of theory that treats totalization—and ideology as its
agent—as the antagonist, we have found literature functioning
as the privileged agent of subversive resistance, indeed, of liberation from the danger of an ideology that would absorb everything into itself. In this tradition there is an insistence, in the
interest of being inclusive rather than exclusive, on using literature to splinter any all-enclosing ideological structure.

However, this conception of literature, as that which can liberate us from the closures of ideology, inverts what had been the
standard attack on formalist critics (since at least the heyday of
the New Criticism) precisely for advocating a literary text's aesthetic closure and hence its totalized and totalizing character. In
recent years we have seen the usual antiformalist attack turn

largely political: tracing formalism back to the rise of organicism in the nineteenth century and forward through its development into the New Criticism in the twentieth, it charged formalists, guilty as they were of organicist commitments, with imposing totalization upon their version of the literary text in its quest for closure. As antiformalism would have it, it was the literary text, as it was defined by organicists, that was to generate a self-sealing form in the dynamic mutuality of all its internal relations, thereby seeking a totalization that excluded everything else. Accordingly, formalists had to condemn all nonfictional discourse because they saw it as unfortunately open to, and ruled by, the world of external generic meanings and hence as lacking the internal completeness of self-sufficiency. It is this common argument—that formalists must conceive of the literary as totalized and exclusive and of the nonliterary as open and inclusive—that I have here been trying to turn around.

The source of this version of the antiformalist argument is, as I have said, found in the emergence of formalism out of nineteenth-century organicism. It was this organicist call for an all-enclosing unity that constituted the basis of the developing discipline of aesthetics in the nineteenth century. It was also this coupling of organicism with the aesthetic, and hence the formal, that antagonistic sociopolitical theorists charge with having reactionary political consequences. These theorists borrow and broaden Walter Benjamin's critique of "the aestheticization of the political," a phrase that haunts current political criticism, which uses it to leap from totalization in discourse to totalitarianism in politics.

According to this argument, the post-Kantian valorization of the aesthetic, because it is supposedly free of worldly "interest," is actually, however surreptitiously, in the service of a very strong interest, that of the existing power structure, which uses the power of the aesthetic to extend its sway.[22] In this way totalization in the aesthetic realm, as the product of organicism, leads to—or rather turns into—totalization, and hence the totalitarian, in the political realm. The organically perfect literary work serves as the humanist's metonymic emblem of the all-mastering, totalitarian state. As in the model of Hegel, organicist as both aesthetician and theorist of history, the aesthetic overruns and transforms the political as more and more complete unities, higher and higher syntheses, force upon every would-be errant particular its obligation to serve the universal, fulfilling its function in a higher unity, model of the nation-state system that turns utterly repressive in asserting its wholeness. And much of postmodern theory has worked toward undoing these totalizations, first aesthetic but ultimately political, which are foisted upon us by such doctrine.

A closer examination of what I have been calling the counter-ideological tradition in theory reveals that, far from calling for a literature of closure, it would have literature, in its duplicity, persistently resist closure. Instead, it would find the agent of closure in ideological theory, as well as in the discourse it sanctions, even though it is just that sort of theory which seeks to indict the aesthetic for imposing closure. Ideological theorists may well be impatient with the complexities of the poetic fiction as it playfully develops itself, because it seems to exclude their interests. However, others I have been treating in this chapter would argue that a careful reading finds those interests addressed, though only as they are exceeded.

So, for the recent version of the counterideological tradition, it is not literature that is seen as the discourse that rests upon the closure of universalizing assumptions, acknowledged or unacknowledged; on the contrary, it is that other sort of discourse, which seems to ask not to be read poetically, that makes its coercive ideological claims upon us, even when, as in its current guises, it would hide its essentialist, metaphysical features. It is the latter discourse, which cannot help but serve ideology, that can be seen as repressive in the closed exclusiveness of its affirmations and denials. And it is the exemption from such a narrow mission, with the consequent indulgence in the space for play, that allows for the potential openness and the liberating effects of a literary text.

It is likely, then, that the attack upon the formal conception of the integral literary text for its totalizing character rests upon false grounds as long as that formal conception retains a counter-ideological character. Such a rethinking of the politics of discourse would persuade us to reverse the anti-aesthetic judgment about which texts are repressive and which texts open themselves to admitting what is otherwise repressed. After all, what could be more *in*clusive than those texts that, as literary texts can, will admit, and give equal status to, the contradictory of any apparent proposition that stakes out an ideological claim? Or, to look at the other side and examine, in this light, the theory that would reject the aesthetic, what could be more *ex*clusive in its totalization than an ideological call to action that would repress anything that gets in the way? The continuing impact of the counterideological reading of texts, as one that sees the literary as free of the logical and rhetorical constraints that discourse normally imposes, rests upon what it grants to the power of irony and, consequently, upon the unrestrained breadth of the materials and conflicting attitudes that literature, with its counterideological license, can admit.

Looked at this way rather than the other way around, totalization is that which the discourse of ideology imposes, and it is that *from* which, potentially, the counterideological discourse of the literary text can liberate us. The emphasis of Foucauldian critics, as New Historicists, has been on the all-devouring power of any one of history's discourse formations. Nothing seems more closed and thus repressive than what Foucault termed an "episteme," a discursive formation that in its time created, ruled over, and was served by all the elements of its languages. Our discourse is totally enclosed by it, and so totally determined by it.

But we must remind ourselves that much of the excitement generated by the early Foucault, as a poststructuralist, came from his insistence on the disruptive openings, the gaps, between "epistemes," those jagged breaks that help to mark the end of one episteme and the beginning of the next. If we can focus upon those creases that are created by the fractures in history's flow, and the role played by literature in bringing them about, then the potential for discursive freedom emerges for us. In contrast to the charge of a closed determinism that I have leveled at theoretical movements that claim to follow Foucault, there is space for this postmodern freedom in Foucault's own earlier texts. Indeed, despite his theory of the controlling episteme, I should have earlier included Foucault with Bakhtin and Lyotard as being among those who press the counterideological tendency in theory to its sociopolitical consequences.

Among Foucault's many commentators, David Carroll, who has studied these epistemic fissures in Foucault's version of our culture's history, has taught me the most. The title of one of Carroll's chapters immediately makes his focus clear: "Disruptive Discourse and Critical Power/Foucault."[23] The chapter carries out the promise of its title. After his discussion of the role Foucault assigns to Diderot's *Rameau's Nephew,* Carroll writes that such disruptive texts "escape categorization and contextualization and remain the only discursive elements not dependent on the episteme of their period" (earlier defined as a period's "languages, institutions, ideologies, and discursive practices"). Disruptive texts "cannot be contained" by the episteme and thus "provide Foucault with a perspective outside each episteme, a perspective from which the episteme that is about to disappear and the one that is about to take over can be described and their 'productions' analyzed." Consequently, as a "leap of discourse beyond discourse" "through certain radical discursive practices," "literature at its most critical may constitute a 'counter-discourse,' as Foucault argues."

What is being claimed, clearly, is that even Foucault, unlike most of those who follow in his name, can be seen—at least in his early work—as privileging the literary text, so that, far from itself being closed, that text is granted the power to violate the predetermined totalization of the governing episteme. By freeing language, breaking through what *is* otherwise closed—breaking through, that is, those unrelenting, repressive structures of thought projected by history's language—it can, according to Foucault, undermine and lead beyond the ruthless totality created by the discourses imposed by a period's ideology.

However, after all that can be said on behalf of the single text as a carnivalizing instrument, as the autonomous fiction that counters any master fiction, and all that can be said on behalf of any theory that argues for such a text, we must worry—even here—about the temptations of universalizing, and hence essentializing, such claims. For even negation itself has no immunity against such temptations. There may well be something self-defeating, or even dangerous, in the suggestion that carnival or subversion or even revolution should function as a permanent, and hence a universal, process; that resistance should be raised to institutional status. The consequence would be to press the anti-systematic into becoming its own system, to counter one ideology with another, even if it is one that ideologizes opposition.[24]

If the subversive is turned into a universal, then the subversive itself has become an ideology and as such will find itself seeking to become a rival institution. It is in the nature of ideologies to find their institutional reflections, and it is in the nature of institutions, I fear, to create themselves even out of anti-institutional motives. The declaration of the resistance to a universal — to any ideology — by any particular in rebellion to it still exposes that particular to the danger that its very resistance can become frozen into a universal. And what then would be the *other,* the counterideological resistance, to the counterideological ideology? To turn the subversive — the counterideological — into an institution with its companion ideology, a negative ideology of "permanent revolution," ironically collapses all differences in the very act of calling for endless differentiation — and *only* differentiation.

This *is* a significant danger and should recall us to our need to maintain some balance between the call for antisystematic subversion and our awareness of what the forgoing of rational system entails. Still, having noted the inevitable danger that accompanies a universal call for resistance against universals, I must observe that in these ideological days it is the pressure to resist, as well as the role of literature in supplying it, that is sorely needed. There may be moments in the history of theory when the counterideological swing becomes so strong as to force us to remind those indulging in it of the danger of their own drift into the ideology of negation. Such a moment exposed to that danger may well have existed, several decades back, under the aegis of late modernism.

That is hardly the situation now; there is currently a far greater danger from the hegemonic rule of ideology, from one political wing or the other, than there is from an ideology of resistance to ideology; a far greater danger from the rejection of the notion of the literary as counterideological than there is from an idolatry of the literary. Against those who would use Foucault to support their commitment to an ideologically based theory, we can say, claiming to speak in his spirit, that our current episteme must *not* become the one in which we seek to freeze ourselves by theorizing ourselves out of the means—that is, the discourse—to break free of it.

Even so, I again must acknowledge the importance of resisting the opposite temptation, which besets those carrying forward the counterideological mission of literature: the temptation to thematize the oppositional elements of the literary text. We must guard against generalizing the carnivalizing resistance that we may read in the text, so that we emerge with a theory proclaiming resistance itself as the universal characteristic of all literature. One has to do quite a balancing act to let loose the counterideological potential of one literary text after another, while resisting the universalizing thematic consequences to which this procedure might lead. But the balance is worth trying to maintain, since such texts can help restore the vigor and the health of the body politic as long as they are interpreted as some of our less extreme counterideological critics have interpreted them: not as a negative ideological alternative to the dominant set of social values, so much as the creators of distrust in those values as the latter are monolithically imposed. Texts that are treated this way become responsive to our need to multiply these values and to complicate their constellations by emphasizing their capacity to thrive in the face of mutual differentiation and opposition.

It may well be that what most makes literature worth studying is what it reveals to us about ideology (as well as negative ideology) by revealing its totalizing dangers to us. Plato may indeed have fostered the theory of imitation that subjected texts to being reflections of outside meanings; but for him, unhappily, they were too often the wrong outside meanings—not those sanctioned by the reasonable order of the state, which had to guard against the dissident attractions of the literary. In the reactionary service of his ideal society, he insisted that the literary, with its endless variety, the restless oppositions within its manifold images, could, because of its powerful appeal, contaminate all discourse and create a subversive threat to the ruling language of his "republic" as a static entity. For this reason Plato, as authoritarian, at times wanted to outlaw the arts for escaping the lofty mimetic role he would have liked them to perform as they indulged the lowly mimetic role that would, in its base appeal, contaminate the state and its discourse.

Recognizing that same power in the arts, I am urging their indispensability—and never more than at the present time. Thinking of the monolithic character of the discourses we are likely to encounter today outside the arts, I can only hope for them to be contaminated by the discourses of the arts. As I have earlier suggested, the literary art performs perhaps its most important service for society by contaminating the reader's other reading experiences: by inducing the compliant reader to learn to read fully, to indulge in the play of the text's language and its fictions, thereby preparing that reader to find this sort of play and these fictions in a great variety of texts, many of them not ostensibly "literary" or "aesthetic."

Thanks to the theoretical tendency whose history I have been tracing, which encourages in literature the resistance to the generic language of ideology, I can reject the metaphor of disease in that word "contaminate" and, instead, find in it an opening outward that contributes to a culture's health. So I conclude by reemphasizing the healthy skepticism produced by the verbal imagination as it has been charted by those who would probe its counterideological tendencies and would resist any easy submission to the veil of Maya. Such theorists are insisting on the power of the text to create beyond what its surrounding discourse has provided, on its power to surprise the compliant reader. And surprise is precisely what the text as read by ideological criticism must lack.

So they would ask readers to be compliant, and thus more submissive to the powers of textuality than historical determinism would allow—precisely because they are to remain open to being surprised by what they find in their reading. Nor is there any need for them to evade the political. On the contrary, in pressing their case, these theorists would seek to secure a connection, at once firm and yet surely *un*reassuring, between the aesthetic and the anthropological as a feature of our political consciousness, which now would have in it some element of resistance to the totalizing force of ideology; not just to this or that ideology, but to the narrows, if not the total enclosure, of the ideological attachment itself. If, after Schiller, we now see that liberating consciousness as itself aesthetic,[25] we can feel a gratification as political creatures in indulging the aesthetic even as we use it to look beyond.

# 4   A Hortatory Conclusion

I BEGAN THIS VOLUME BY TRACING THE ACADEMIC COMMITMENT
to theory: its emergence out of the intense practice of literary
criticism after that criticism had earlier flourished as the antagonistic successor to traditional historical scholarship. In this past
half-century we have seen theory move from an auxiliary role, in
which it sought to justify the practice of literary criticism, to the
status of a self-conscious discipline, and then into its imperialistic phase, in which it would doom that which it had been created
to protect. For clearly, in the development of the theoretical enterprise into what is the present industry of theory, we have seen the
extent to which it has become increasingly antagonistic to the
practice of literary criticism.

My own career has run parallel to these developments in
their earlier stages, springing as it has from my original attempt
to put theory into the controlling position I thought it should
have in literary studies, so that it could weigh and put in place
the roles of criticism and history as it sought to make systematic
sense of the creation and reception of literary texts. In accord
with the title of this book, I was unwittingly promoting nothing
less than the institution of theory, though only for the sake of
enhancing our understanding of literature itself and its function
in the human economy.

At the outset of my career, theory in the American academy
was in a nascent stage, without power and with very little recog-
nition. Even the New Criticism, a movement that was the major
influence on my early work, preferred not to look into its relation
to theory. At such a moment of neglect, I could not then antic-
ipate that, in pressing for the just claims of theory, I was setting
in motion forces that, once let loose, would impose themselves

imperialistically upon all the discourses of the "human sciences," even to the point of dissolving the self-privileging claims of literary texts and their defenders.

I concede that, almost forty years ago, when I first undertook my own early battles on behalf of theory against a recalcitrant scholarly establishment—against, that is, the institution of the sort of historical scholarship I now refer to as the Old Historicism—I did so primarily in order to press theory's special claims on behalf of the workings of literature. I identified theory with the "apology for poetry," which had assumed a number of forms throughout the history of criticism, and I saw myself as a "new apologist." Behind my aggressive defense of what was then termed *poetics* was the assumption that there was then a special need for theory to be pushed forward aggressively so that it could let loose the repressed power of poetry—because I saw that it *was* poetry whose power was being repressed by what I have been calling the Old Historicism.

However ambitious I was for theory, my efforts on its behalf, I now know, were to be self-limiting: I thought I was intending theory to be an instrument, not an institution. I hardly intended to replace one institution with another—the institution of historicism with the institution of theory—while poetry would suffer from one not much less than from the other. But subsequent developments have carried theory far beyond my intention, and with others I—and my culture—now have to face the consequences. I could not, in my early struggles on behalf of theory, be aware of the extent to which, by becoming a rival institution to historicism, it could develop the potential eventually to inhibit, if not to stifle, the poetry that it had been supposed to set free.

So my championing of theory was originally limited to the service of the literary functions of the text that historical scholars were not giving a chance to display themselves, so anxious were they to press only the text's historical—and hence derivative and reflective—function. But, as I have argued at greater length in Chapter 1, once theory, as a generalizing discipline, went into business for itself and itself became an institution, it had to reduce, or attempt to reduce, all that the individual literary text might perform, in order to prevent that text from displaying any powers that might subvert the a priori claims of a theory. In a number of places in my work I have referred to this excess, or diversion or subversion, in literary texts as "those more things on heaven and earth" than are dreamt of in any theorist's philosophy.[1] I have seen the poem and its antireductive interpreters as playing Hamlet to the theorist's Horatio. Perhaps from the beginning I should have been more wary of the potential antagonism between the claims of poetry and the claims of theory, unless a theory could be cultivated that, in self-denial, would declare its need to give way before the performance of the poem.

In my early book *The Play and Place of Criticism* (1967), I worked toward a criticism and a theory that, at the risk of being paradoxical, would fix a place for poetry while allowing it the freedom to play within that place. And, as late as my *Theory of Criticism: A Tradition and Its System* (1976), I tried to respect the tension that exists, and should exist, between literary theory and the literary work by acknowledging the "limits" necessarily placed on the "capacities" of theory to contain the individual works it would account for; by acknowledging, in other words, the "vanity" as well as the "value" of theory. By reserving for the literary text the chance to provoke a radically new response, unanticipated by a prior theory that would seek in vain to account for it in advance, I must confess that I was conferring a unique privilege upon what the internal complexities of a literary text might perform. But, alas, theory now sees "privilege" as the self-exposing word whose metaphorical implications open such thinking to the ravages of the political critique, which sees in it the self-protective prejudices of those who are socially empowered.

In its allegiance to organicism, the theory of reading and evaluation behind the practice of the New Criticism exclusively privileged the internal manipulations of the language of the individual literary work. In so doing it was implicitly arguing for the power of the poem to thwart, by exceeding, any bounds set for it by the universal characterizations of any theory; in other words, arguing for the power of the poem to surprise even the most theoretically armed reader. The task of the interpreter-critic was to perform the poem, or rather to allow the poem to perform itself: to set free its uniqueness, its newness, which any prior theory would force into the channels of a more generic discourse. Thus the critic arrogated to himself or herself an extraordinary and indispensable role, that of playing the middleman-interpreter between the poem and the reader, while resisting falling into the universalizing traps of the theorist. This was the function that the critic, specially equipped, was to fulfill in bringing the work—as R. P. Blackmur put it—to its full performance potential by bringing "to consciousness the means of performance."[2] Despite the conservative and classical instincts of the New Critics, theirs was an unabashed romantic defense of the poem's potential originality, of its power, through what it performs, to make culture even while it appears to have been made by culture.

The New Critics were often charged with self-aggrandizement in urging a theory of reading that, by elevating the single work into a sacred mystery of which they were the self-appointed priests, made their own function indispensable, as we have seen in my reference to Blackmur. Devoted as they were to poetic complications, and thus bestowing the highest value upon the most intricately patterned works, they argued, in the wake of T. S. Eliot, for poetry's need to be "difficult." So strongly did they press the need to find complexities in the interpretation of poems whose "difficulties" they insisted on searching out that the belletristic establishment, doubting that poetry was as complex as they would have it, attacked them under the group name "the cult of obscurantism," a stigma that today may sound familiar. The New Critics seemed to be arguing, in a self-inflating and self-serving way, for a poetry that needed the critic to probe within it for us, a poetry that could not merely stand on its own before the common reader. This was indeed a priestly function. If poems were to be evaluated in proportion to their difficulty, then for the best of them we would need the critic (that is, those uncommon readers trained to be New Critics) to explicate their complexities. The cultural need for this sort of critic as teacher would be assured.

I concede that this charge, beyond its being one among the many anti–New Critical weapons being wielded for some time now, may be worth thinking about seriously, as having an impact upon theory. To require the interpretive apparatus of the critic to read a poem tells us something about the special, otherwise undecipherable, way in which poems speak. It is a way that would elude the dictatorial forms of our usual speech, our easy historical generalizations, and the universal pretensions of theory. If we grant the ideological character of theory on the one side, and on the other the counterideological propensities that much of our critical tradition has bestowed upon the literary, then the argument for literary complexity can be seen as just another of the many versions of the argument, which I have traced across the centuries in Chapter 3, for poetry's potential to undermine the language of any theory or any historical epoch that, by predetermining the poem, would limit its reach.

The only theory that would tolerate this claim of the poem's counterideological power is one that would undo both itself and the very theoretical urge, by acknowledging its own impotence before all that the poem performs, all that it makes happen on its own.[3] Such a theory would empower poetry to undermine the no-longer-altogether determining forces of history, as well as the universalizing claims of theory, even while poetry is *partly* explained by both of them. But only partly, and for the more modest theory the "partly" is not strong enough to account for, or to preclude, poetry's performative power, which calls for the specially trained perceptions of the critic.

However, the version of theory that we have been watching emerge during these past decades was far less modest and self-effacing as it pressed forward with its imperialistic ambitions. In its present institutional role, that sort of theory would overwhelm the full performance potential of the individual poem no less than historicism did when it took the form of the Old Historicism that first prompted, by way of opposition, the rise of the early *literary* theory that would authorize the New Critics to unleash poetry's powers.

More recently, as an addendum to this narrative of theory's fortunes, theory has been having its own struggle for survival against the resurrected dominion of historicism, whose all-reducing determinism threatens to undermine the universalizing pretensions that have guided theory's rise to institutional power. I am defining historicism, old or new, as a mode of interpretation that inflates sociohistorical contingency until it is seen as the universally exclusive shaper of our discourse — until it becomes what

Aristotle would have deemed a "sufficient" as well as a "necessary" cause of all we write. Thus the transformation of the discipline of history into the dogma of historicism, despite the latter's distrust of the transhistorical claims of theory, elevates historical causality to theoretical status, carrying with it all of theory's hegemonic pretensions against which historicism complains. Nevertheless, the reborn historicist industry gains much of its impetus because of its claim to replace the theory industry. By introducing the one universal of contingency, historicism argues that in its newer form it precludes the possibility of theory, thereby delegitmating theory as we have known it and ushering in what it sees as a post-theoretical period.

This recently renewed dedication to the relativizing hand of historical contingency would, of course, undermine poetry no less than theory, so that both poetry and theory are now struggling to defend themselves against the claims of New Historicism, even in its more sophisticated guise of neopragmatism. Not only would theory as we have known it lose its license, but poetry would be at least as disenfranchised by this historicism as it was by theory in its over-reaching moments. Of course, apologists for poetry would argue that the literary way of dealing with language shows its resistance to the one, history, as freely as it does to the other, theory. So, whatever the mutually destructive rivalry recently generated between theory and historicism, it is a combat in which poetry can have little stake, because recent history demonstrates that it cannot hope to be empowered by either, even as it resists both. But, as a postlude to the institution of theory, I have to examine that rivalry and its consequences.

From the eighteenth century until now, we can observe a succession of oscillations between the dominance of theory at the expense of historicism and the dominance of historicism at the expense of theory. These have been oscillations between approaches built on spatial models to the exclusion of historical contingencies, and approaches built on temporal models to the exclusion of transhistorical universals. The philosophic urge to universalize our experiences sometimes has overpowered, and sometimes has been overpowered by, our awareness of contingency, of the temporal flow of our experience, which is constantly differentiating itself.

Hence one kind of distrust, our distrust of the philosopher's claim that we can attain a standing from which we can transcend the time in which we — always a differentiated "we" — drift along, is matched by another, opposed sort of distrust, our Socratic distrust of the historicist who would doom us to a Heraclitean flux. Spatializing theorists have reified the common elements they presume to find, whereas historicizing skeptics have worried about the constraints those theorists have had to impose upon the always differentiated moments that they want to merge into that commonality. Historicists have deconstructed the theorist's universal by subjecting it to the contingencies of the self-differentiating moment, but could do so only by universalizing the dominion of the culturally relative. So perhaps even in the extremes of historicism the temporal has been captured by the spatial, the historicist by the theorist within.

I have pointed out that, in its current form, the struggle between the rival institutions of theory and historicism, which I have suggested may well be viewed as just another struggle between rival theoretical institutions, seems to have proceeded with the undisputed understanding by both sides that the literary has no distinctive license. In this agreement the combatants reveal that they are participating in a single swing of a second succession of oscillations that we have undergone these past two centuries: that between moments in which the literary is the subject of a romantic idolatry because of the special visionary power it is granted, and moments in which the literary is taken as just one among many manifestations of a culture, without special entitlements. These days both theorists and historicists usually join in the second of these, often even to the point of claiming that the category "literary" no longer has any authority or even, perhaps, any meaning, beyond being the projection of an elitist's nostalgic wish. With a contempt reminiscent of Thomas Love Peacock's *Four Ages of Poetry* (1820), the protective attitude toward the literary is declared obsolete.

To propose that what is happening is only an oscillation in an extended series of oscillations is itself, of course, to take the long historical view. As I have suggested elsewhere, the historian might well unite with the theorist as joint ironists in asking, with Shakespeare, the double-edged question, "Whether revolution be the same."[4] Embedded in the question is the ambiguity of "revolution," a single substantive extension of the two very different verbs, "revolt" and "revolve," thereby suggesting at once utter disruption *and* bland continuity, both a breakthrough of the different *and* just more of the same.

The exhilaration surrounding a new conception that claims to transform for good all that had been thought is greatly diminished by the suggestion that we are only engaging in the repetition of what has gone before. Yet every revolutionary movement is encompassed by the rhetoric that would expunge, or at least radically revise, all that has preceded it through the centuries. Indulging the myth of progress as a narrative form that is more spatial than temporal, the self-proclaimed new movement announces with its advent the end of the history of error. Even when the appeal is to a historicity that proclaims no constancy except the constancy of change, it carries the implication that it has arrived at the final truth and that theoretical history can at last have a stop.

Of course history does not have a stop. Nor is it always necessarily moving upward as it moves onward. Nor, if we are to believe historicist arguments, is history moving in accordance with *any* definable shape, lest it also be subject to a theoretics of space. Still, one cannot historicize away all theory except by using a historicist model that itself turns out to be theoretical. So the attack by historicism on the possibility of theory—the denial of the very theoretical urge, as some sort of transhistorical, universalizing impulse—is made from a self-indicting position once historicism itself proves to be just another theory. Even if, in self-defense, one claims that historicism is only a method rather than a theory, it must be asked whether anyone, Deconstructionist or Historicist, can have a method that does not, almost by its own momentum, grow into a transhistorical theory; and then whether there can be any theory that does not, at some point, persuade its propagator to essentialize, and hence to thematize, it into an implicit metaphysic. Put this way, the questions themselves imply the response.

Any essentialized theoretical program (including the historicist program, I now can say) imposes severe limits on a text whose emerging language system, wrapped in fictionality, would generate potential meanings beyond the a priori predictions of the program. The history of literature is the story of certain texts (and, happily, their number and their sources, especially in recent days, are being constantly and often radically enlarged) that remain teasingly out there, with a fullness in a part or the whole of them that challenges all we think we have known until we meet them; that keeps them beyond the confining reach of anything that theory and history have allowed us to bring to them; that contradicts all efforts to level them into common discourse.

It is, then, hardly enough to replace theory as an institution with historical contingency as an institution because the latter also precludes the independently generative power of the text. The universal pretensions of theory are countermanded not only by historicist contingency, but also—together with historical commonplaces—by the holdout pressure of every resistant text. Theory should again be called upon to protect the literary text's resistance against ideology's repression, even though it is alien to theory's own universalizing interests to do so. It is not easy. The text as anti-ideological is, in its antiuniversal dedication, anti-institutional: a theory that elevates the text (and the act of reading it) to the institutional level has an anti-institutional safeguard—its commitment to resistance—built into it. As an institution, this sort of theory would be resisting its own institutional ideology in order to find a suppleness to match that of its endlessly restive subjects. In other words, theory must resist enjoying the institutional status it has achieved, but can do so only by bowing to the countertheoretical pressure of the poem. In this self-denying mood, it may discover its answer to historicism as well.

Such a theory bids that we hold it lightly, so that we can return to the text, reading as free agents, open to being surprised by a verbal sequence that we can endow with the seductions of a fictional containment that resists whatever we bring with us to capture—to contain—it with. And we have been taught that there are many texts besides what are called "literary" texts upon which we can work—or do we allow them to work?—such an all-disarming magic. Where the freedom of a self-conscious fiction encourages the play of action, of characters, of trope, of language, it gives literature (or at least what we read as literature) a special — I dare say privileged — place among the discourses, because it leads us to read momentary excursions into the literary by the other kinds of discourse: literature proper thus functions as a model for our reading the others, in part or whole, as literary. In this way, too, the study of the literary can resist any self-enclosures and can break beyond any discursive boundaries, though only while it continues to cherish the uniqueness of its own project.

Mine is a plea for theory to reengage the lingering promise of the aesthetic, despite all that has been said to delegitmate it, and to provide a place for a literary theory again. Of course we no longer speak today of aesthetic "objects" as if, in some ontological sense, they had the requisite characteristics *in* them, whether we choose to discover or ignore them. Instead, we speak of a reader's or an observer's receptivity that has been shaped by a set of expectations about what should be there for that reader. It is that receptivity that I hope will open up to the aesthetic, which, in the verbal arts, is to say the literary fiction, whose self-consciousness as fiction has been constituted as a conventional pattern that our cultural tradition, in its aesthetic mode, has made available to our responsiveness.

The literary may function as this self-conscious fiction as long as the reader (in response to what is taken to be the text's encouragement) chooses to read it that way. And different readers may well argue about which texts, or portions of texts — ostensibly poetic or not — do or do not encourage such a reading, though we must be careful not to rule any of them in or out on merely generic grounds. For those of us anxious to preserve this way of reading, in distinction to others, the power we claim to find in any of these texts is related to our willingness to indulge its capacity to move us beyond the demarcations of its historically ordained period values — related, that is, to the counterideological way we read it.

We have become accustomed, these days, to find that many texts, long revered on these grounds, are now condemned by being reduced to unsavory political motives, conscious or unconscious. Their literary capacity is being dissolved into the ugly political ramifications of discursive practices they may well have absorbed from the language habits that surround them. And surely it must be granted that many literary works we have long admired were composed and appreciated under political conditions we now properly find most indefensible. Does it necessarily follow that our affection for these texts is now to be demystified, and perhaps altogether abandoned? that these texts are themselves similarly indefensible? This would be the case only if they did not go beyond reflecting the sociopolitical world around them. But instead, can we not still read them closely enough to discover how much of what we now detest in the value system that surrounds them is being challenged and even undercut by what we find in them? And can we not then admire them still?

What, after all, can be more repressive than the wholesale rejection, or rejection piece by piece, of texts whose richness has functioned as literary for other historical moments (up to as recently, perhaps, as three decades ago), simply by taking criteria from current ideology, bestowing universal authority upon them, and then applying them retroactively upon those texts? Does not this rejection display an arrogance, a lack of self-awareness, that rests on the exemption of ourselves from the historical and political contingencies that we insist upon for all others? My complaint might be answered by an insistence that until now, with the current strain of right thinking that we pride ourselves on sharing, no historical moment, and hence no one until us, had got it right. Such a naïve attachment to the idea of progress implies, if it does not say explicitly, that latest is best: that our history of thinking and writing is the history of ignorance and error—and worse, of prejudice and oppression. Would it even then follow that our literary works of the past are just as inferior to what, from our privileged position, is now being produced? One would not have much difficulty in producing empirical evidence to the contrary, I fear.[5]

Too many current interpretations are stunted by the desire to bring down older works by tracing them to predictable political causes and finding them productive of predictable political consequences, from both ends thinning their meaning. These only make more evident the need for the interpreter to indulge readings that allow the potential in the text for the resistance to ideology to display itself. This indulgence can occur only to the extent that the reader grants to the text the freedom to play with the givens of its inherited discourse, a freedom that derives from a fictional, and hence aesthetic, separateness from what is usually expected of discourse.

Among the arts, the literary may be the most vulnerable version of the aesthetic because it depends upon a material, just words, that is the common vehicle of all discourse: it can wear any privilege bestowed upon it only through an act of faith by the bestower. And it is the self-consciousness of those projected fictions as aesthetic entities that induces us to make that act of faith. In making it, we would have to respond to the literary play of language that leads us to avoid the monolithic; that allows this language, as we open ourselves to it, to complicate itself in ways to which Deconstructionists have newly alerted us. Through this sort of reading we open ourselves to a verbal world that, through excess, transgresses what our language, as forced upon us by our culture and by our theories, has until then provided for our vision. That vision, moral and political as well as aesthetic, is redefined accordingly. And so is our language, sometimes even to the point of rewriting the language of our cultures.

The language of a culture has constantly to be rewritten if it is to be responsive to the intricacies of our consciousness, which resist the attempts of the existing cultural discourse to represent them. It is the failure of our usual sort of verbal representation that makes verbal representation in its several disfiguring, but highly figured, forms anthropologically necessary. In the literary text, words are, after all, not about themselves—as Deconstructionist theory these days is too often, and often inaccurately, charged with saying—but about that in the world of our consciousness, of our inner experience, which ordinarily resists being represented by them. The extraordinary text, or the extraordinary in texts, manages, for those who read for the extraordinary, to come close to opening that world for us.

My argument may well be just another plea to allow a chance for the extraordinary particular, which is not already contained within a ruling universal, to disclose what without it we could not have anticipated. I look forward wistfully—though not hopefully, I fear—to a criticism in which sociohistorical and literary critics make common cause in illuminating a culture's consciousness, not by resting in the more secure assertions found in its other discourses, but by searching out those problematic clusters of meaning complexes that only literary discourse—or discourse read as literary—can yield. How can literary texts find the freedom to generate attitudes toward ideology, or counterideology, if they themselves are ideology-determined? The answer may be found in the special configurations of their language—which also encompasses both figuration and disfiguration—as it has been made historically available, but also as it has been manipulated by the subject as author. Must we abandon the hope for human subjects, by means of such texts, to drive history, once we concede the extent to which it is history and its institutions, with their ideological basis, that drive our texts, and us by means of them? Despite the persuasive challenge that historicism in its political mode presses upon literature, can a theory of reading ignore the power we grant to literature to expose the existential paradoxes at the base of the human condition of every subject, regardless of the specific political context?

This may hardly seem the time, given recent tendencies in theory and historicism alike, to put forward the power of the subject—by way of a transcendental self, post-Kantian style— because that vision has been rejected as a self-delusion cultivated to protect the bourgeois dream of a private freedom. But how can we attribute to the text, during the scrupulous act of our reading it, such powers as I have suggested, without reintroducing the authority of human consciousness—yes, the exiled human subject—despite the denials that acute epistemological and semiotic skepticism has recently and often persuasively imposed upon us? This consciousness must, more than ever today, seek to contain multitudes—still the multitudes that Walt Whitman's ego would contain—even while watching them disperse into historical contingencies. Or is this not to confess that, perhaps, as Frank Lentricchia charged, mine *is* "the last romanticism" after all?[6]

Nor may this be the final irony that history visits upon me. As I look back over the many years and books to the start of my career, now four decades ago, I hope my argument has grown and changed, or at least that it has thickened with qualifications, so that it rests on very different grounds from those from which it emerged originally. Still, how should I respond if one were to turn the words of my own earliest title against me now and charge me with being, after all these years and books, a renewed apologist for poetry?

Guilty.

# Notes

CHAPTER 1. Institutionalizing Theory

1. I had to remark also that *culture* has become a rather magic, if politically loaded, word in the United States during these last years, although hardly in the limited sense of the term made familiar to us for many decades by anthropologists. I had just learned that the institute I was addressing was shortly to receive a new name, in which the word *culture* was to be replaced by the word *studies*. In the United States, I said, things were moving in the opposite direction, because, with *culture* having become a sacred term, it would be more likely to be used to replace *studies* in giving title to an entity than the other way around. But that is part of the story I was to tell, and am to tell here, part of the history of *our* politics and *our* institutions.

2. In my book of that title, *Words about Words: Theory, Criticism, and the Literary Text* (Baltimore: Johns Hopkins University Press, 1988).

3. I must own up to my own earlier book that used those words in its title, *Theory of Criticism: A Tradition and Its System* (Baltimore: Johns Hopkins University Press, 1976). In it my notion of theory had the restrictions I am describing here.

4. It is true that textualist Deconstruction forms a major and widely influential movement that comes between the heyday of the New Criticism and the various versions of the New Historicism that are dominant today. But it is these latter that not only complete the expulsion of the literary but also insist upon a broad and multidisciplinary domain of psychosocial theory that would claim the center of academic power.

Throughout these chapters, I use the phrase "New Historicism" to cover a far broader variety of theorists than those (represented most prominently by Stephen Greenblatt and the *Representations* group and their Americanist allies) to whom that name is most narrowly applied. I prefer this blanket usage even if it verges on inaccuracy with respect to what various groups call themselves. The poststructuralist attempt to return to explanation by historical contingency, though always through an intense concern with language, characterizes Neo-Marxist, Cultural Materialist, Feminist, various minoritist, and Gay and Lesbian theorists, all of whom—to the extent that they are also poststructuralists—have some indebtedness to Foucault's view of "discourse formations."

5. This phrase is the heart of Fredric Jameson's book *The Political Unconscious: Narrative as a Socially Symbolic Act* (Ithaca: Cornell University Press, 1981), especially his lengthy first chapter (pp. 17–102).

CHAPTER 2. Two Faces of an Old Argument

1. We can also see in this argument only a newer version of the opposition I discussed earlier between Tory and Whig criticism, between those who encouraged imitation and those who wanted only original genius.

2. The essay was published in the *Kenyon Review* 1 (1939): 251–56.

3. My allusion is obviously to the title of a book by Yvor Winters: *Primitivism and Decadence: A Study of American Experimental Poetry* (New York: Arrow Editions, 1937). It was Winters, I should add, who in the same spirit provided to modernist criticism the major distinction between the native English and the borrowed Italianate styles in the English Renaissance lyric, praising those "plain-style" poets who resisted the elegant, ornamental Continental influences. See his "The Sixteenth Century Lyric in England," *Poetry* 53 (1939): 258–72, 320–35; 54 (1939): 35–51.

4. In this emphasis on the differentness of the American experience and, hence, of American literature, this argument anticipates the anticanonical championing today of texts produced by marginal cultures. However, unlike the earlier struggles for the unified vision of *an* American literature, true to *the* American experience, recent movements have adapted their arguments to their vision of a multiplicity of American experiences matching the diversity of a fractured, multicultural society. I cannot overemphasize the importance of this difference.

5. The major theorist responsible for this turn was Hayden White, who, from his early work, *Metahistory* (1972), and the later *Tropics of Discourse* (1978), led the way for a rethinking of the narratological and tropological basis of history as discourse.

6. Among many other places in his work, see Stephen Greenblatt, "Capitalist Culture and the Circulatory System," in *The Aims of Representation: Subject/Text/History,* ed. Murray Krieger (New York: Columbia University Press, 1987), pp. 257–73.

7. I have already acknowledged (see chap. 1, n. 4) that I mean to expand the domain of the New Historicism to include Cultural, Neo-Marxist, Feminist, minoritist, and Gay and Lesbian theorists, along with the Foucauldian group we associate with the Berkeley journal *Representations*. Despite vast differences in objectives and emphases among them, they share an ultimate dependence on the assertion and repressiveness of sociopolitical power, and they impose that dependence upon the texts they treat.

8. In Chapter 3 I will argue, though postdeconstructively, for the distinc-

tion between the kind of deconstructive act that occurs when responding to a text that has elements of poetic fictions in it and the kind of deconstructive act that occurs when responding to a text that is—"nonpoetically"—ostensibly addressed to more unilinear objectives. In the former we can simply follow the poem's self-deconstructive lead, but in the latter we must deconstruct the set of unilinear intentions that controls the usual predeconstructive reading: deconstruct it by reading "against the grain," thereby bringing the text from its origin in the subject-author's intentionality into the open realm of textuality. My suggestion gives a priority to the poem as that which has taught the deconstructive reading technique to the commentator for use on other texts. But this is my distinction, not one that would be acknowledged in these terms by Deconstructionists.

9. It is important to make clear the wide-ranging meaning—well beyond a single, discrete verbal work or a book—that Deconstruction, in the wake of Derrida, means to give to "text" and "textuality." The strength of Derrida's appeal rests on this special sense of "text" that appears repeatedly in his work and that he believes leaves a door open to the political for him. He resents those who would claim that it must be closed. He makes a strongly polemical defense of this broad sense of "text" (as an ever-enlarging semiotic realm hardly restricted to the single verbal sequence we usually refer to as "a text") in his "Critical Response II: But, beyond . . . (Open Letter to Anne McClintock and Rob Nixon)," trans. Peggy Kamuf, *Critical Inquiry* 13 (Autumn 1986): 155–70, esp. 167–70.

10. I must, for my summarizing purposes here, resist the temptation of saying, rather, that it gives all power to the free-wheeling creativity of the reader.

CHAPTER 3. The Ideological Imperative and Counterideological Resistance

1. I remind the reader that New Historicists, because they are committed to a poststructuralist semiotic, would deny that "life," or the social context of a particular historical moment, can be referred to in language as an unproblematic, neutral fixed point of reference in order to explain the less stable signs of a literary text. See my discussion of this issue in Chapter 2, above.

2. This didactic appeal can easily be—and in recent years has easily been—demystified into the revelation that what is being appealed to are not any universal moral truths that are embedded in the nature of things (although this is what is often being claimed), but only the projections of the need of those holding (or seeking) power in order to make certain propositions obligatory and to make the literary work serve those propositions by reflecting them in its individual fictions: life as it ought to be, though only for those who must have it that way. Of course, the appeal to "the nature of things" is the metaphysical claim that calls for deconstruction.

3. The "Neo-Humanists" and the Marxists of the thirties and forties came from opposite ends of the political spectrum to join in the methodologically similar claim that literary works should be seen as no more than allegories of the ideological visions that they would have each fiction serve. Such visions are latent within the cultural context as the structures of power create and shape that context, provided some group with power or some group seeking power could only have its way.

4. Besides the different but overlapping models of subtextuality drawn from Marx and Foucault, which in different ways serve the politics of power (in the case of Marx economic class power), the Lacanian model may also be invoked to reflect the promptings of private desire. But this psychoanalytical one can also, through language as an expression of Jameson's political unconscious, be made to reinforce the sociopolitical model.

5. I must confess to borrowing the window-to-mirror allegory from a very early book of mine, *A Window to Criticism: Shakespeare's* Sonnets *and Modern Poetics* (Princeton: Princeton University Press, 1964).

6. Of course, later Neo-Platonists, by changing the poem's object of imitation from the worldly to the ideal, found a way for the mimetic poet, by aiming at "poetic justice," to be didactic in a way that would have satisfied Plato.

7. In the often-cited chapter 14 of *Biographia Literaria* (1817).

8. Among other places throughout their work, see Schopenhauer, *The World as Will and Idea* (1819); Nietzsche, *The Birth of Tragedy* (1871); and Bergson, *Laughter: An Essay on the Meaning of the Comic* (1900).

9. Again in chapter 14 of his *Biographia Literaria*.

10. See especially Arnold's "The Study of Poetry" (1880), which seeks to find an indispensable role for poetry outside the cognitive role of science. I discuss this aspect of Arnold's thought in "The Critical Legacy of Matthew Arnold: or, The Strange Brotherhood of T. S. Eliot, I. A. Richards, and Northrop Frye," which is reprinted in my *Poetic Presence and Illusion: Essays in Critical History and Theory* (Baltimore: Johns Hopkins University Press, 1979).

11. This distinction occurs throughout the early Richards. See especially his *Science and Poetry* (New York: W. W. Norton and Co., 1926).

12. I. A. Richards, *Principles of Literary Criticism* (London: Routledge and Kegan Paul, 1924), p. 250.

13. The more obvious "model New Critic" might seem to be John Crowe Ransom, who gave the movement its name and momentum with his book, *The New Criticism* (Norfolk, Conn.: New Directions, 1941). Ransom goes further than Richards or Brooks because of his explicitly anti-Platonic and anti-Hegelian insistence on the poem's freedom from the realm of action and action's univocal, all-subjecting discourse. For Ransom the poem indulges a discourse that permits itself to have "texturally" rich "meanderings" from the strict paths of "logical" meaning in order to engage

the world of things in its fullness. It thus escapes the totalitarian control that we associate with the language of science or of action. Ransom himself observes the importance of the political metaphor: "It was the political way of thinking which gave me the first analogy which seemed valid." Unlike discourse under the Platonic and Hegelian dispensation, "the poem was like a democratic state, in action, and observed both macroscopically and microscopically." (The passage is from "Criticism as Pure Speculation," a frequently reprinted essay that first appeared in 1940 as a preview of the arguments pursued in *The New Criticism* a year later.) But, however free Ransom's poem is from the control of "Platonic" or "Hegelian" discourse, the ideological and thus the counterideological are not really his primary concern.

14. Among many places in Cleanth Brooks, see especially "The Problem of Belief and the Problem of Cognition," in *The Well-Wrought Urn* (New York: Reynal and Hitchcock, 1947), pp. 226–38.

15. This quest is usually associated with an organicism attributed to the followers of Coleridge (often cited by them as the author of the definition of imagination as "the balance or reconciliation of opposite or discordant qualities"—*Biographia Literaria,* chap. 14). I have elsewhere tried at length to argue that organicism, once carefully examined, can be shown to be addressing itself as much to a continual dispersal as to the drive to an ultimate unity. Notions like irony in the New Criticism can similarly be seen as pointing both ways, functioning as shotgun as well as arrow. My association of this kind of criticism with the counterideological, so crucial to the argument of this essay, depends on reading the organicist's irony as pointing both ways. I present this revisionist reading of the organicist tradition behind the New Criticism in my *A Reopening of Closure: Organicism against Itself* (New York: Columbia University Press, 1989).

16. Paul de Man, "The Epistemology of Metaphor," *Critical Inquiry* 5 (1978): 13–30. Besides Locke, in this essay de Man similarly takes on Condillac and Kant, two others who represent the extreme version of apparently straightforward, logical, unambiguous, and "unpoetic" thinking.

17. Not that there are not differences of emphases even where similarities of interpretive strategies appear. A recent posthumous collection of de Man's essays contains the comments he delivered in 1981 to a paper of mine in which I dealt briefly with Keats's "Ode to a Nightingale." He specifies his disagreement—within areas of agreement—with my reading of this poem. The difference between our readings rests upon his greater emphasis upon a disruptive moment that we both find in the poem's fiction. But while I seek to reabsorb that moment, he insists that its disruptive force remains intact and should be allowed to leave the poem torn asunder. I am referring to his "Murray Krieger: A Commentary," in his *Romanticism and Contemporary Criticism: The Gauss Seminar and Other Papers,* ed. E. S. Burt, Kevin Newmark, and Andrzej Warminski (Baltimore: Johns Hopkins University Press,

1993), pp. 181–87. The essay of mine that he is discussing is "'A Waking Dream': The Symbolic Alternative to Allegory," reprinted in my *Words about Words about Words: Theory, Criticism, and the Literary Text* (Baltimore: Johns Hopkins University Press, 1988), pp. 271–88.

18. I must in fairness add that de Man did more, in differing from the New Criticism, than treat all texts in ways that New Critics reserved for the special structures of language that they called literary. His war on unity of meaning, which allowed him to find common ground among texts that we used to think of as nonliterary as well as literary, also led him to argue for the openness of all texts, an openness to other texts, indeed to textuality at large. It is this insistence about texts, that none are closed, which for him justifies the search for similar dispersive rhetorical principles among them.

19. Wolfgang Iser, "Representation: A Performative Act," in *The Aims of Representation: Subject/Text/History,* ed. Murray Krieger (New York: Columbia University Press, 1987), esp. p. 221.

20. I take the word *mandarin* from Frank Lentricchia, who uses it, as he does the word *hedonist,* to characterize those critical aesthetes who are guilty of what he treats as asocial escapism (see *After the New Criticism* (Chicago: University of Chicago Press, 1980).

21. In making this qualified statement, I am thinking primarily of Bakhtin, whose interest in the dialogical character of literature focused on the single genre — or for him, antigenre — of the novel.

22. It is largely for this reason that Bertolt Brecht pleads with audiences to resist the theater of illusion, which uses the aesthetic to enhance the hold of bourgeois society upon them.

23. Chapter 5 of David Carroll's *Paraesthetics: Foucault/Lyotard/Derrida* (New York: Methuen, 1987), pp. 107–29. The quotations that follow are taken from pp. 112–17.

24. I deal with this dangerous temptation in "From Theory to Thematics: The Ideological Underside of Recent Theory," in *Words about Words about Words,* pp. 43–63. See esp. pp. 50–57, in which I deal with the ideological implications of the counterideological apology for poetry, including my own.

25. I am referring, of course, to Schiller's *Letters on the Aesthetic Education of Man* (1795).

CHAPTER 4. A Hortatory Conclusion

1. Most recently, I must confess, this allusion appears in Chapter 3 above.

2. R. P. Blackmur, "The Critic's Job of Work," *Hudson Review* 1 (1948): 171.

3. What I am saying here is similar to Hillis Miller's continual insistence, in his recent writings on the "performative" power of literature, that

the text has the power to "make something happen." This is a strong way of seeing its force as primary, not relegating it to a mere reflection of a performative power lodged elsewhere, whether in theory or history.

4. In my essay "Literary Invention, Critical Fashion, and the Impulse to Theoretical Change: 'Or Whether Revolution Be the Same,'" in *Words about Words about Words: Theory, Criticism, and the Literary Text* (Baltimore: Johns Hopkins University Press, 1988), pp. 64–89. The quotation (more completely, the sentence reads "Whether we are mended, or where better they, / Or whether revolution be the same") is taken from Shakespeare's Sonnet 59, "If there be nothing new, but that which is / Hath been before." Like all who have been concerned about the optimistic myth of progress on the one hand and the cynical acceptance of eternal return on the other, the speaker is asking whether the present truly represents an improvement over the past or "whether revolution be the same." True to the Petrarchan convention, he concludes—though this is hardly supportive of my concerns—by affirming the superiority of his beloved despite his skeptical awareness.

5. For more of this argument, I refer the reader to my essay "The Arts and the Idea of Progress," reprinted in *Words about Words about Words,* pp. 20–42.

6. Frank Lentricchia, "Murray Krieger's Last Romanticism," in *After the New Criticism* (Chicago: University of Chicago Press, 1980), pp. 212–54.

# Index